Benson's Animal Farm

Lynne Ober

GoJo Venture

Published by GoJo Venture, New Hampshire

Copyright © by Lynne Ober
All rights reserved

First Published in 2010

Manufactured in the United States

ISBN 978-0-578-05785-951799

Note: The information in this book is true and complete to the best of the author's knowledge. It is offered without guarantee on the part of the author or the publisher. The author and the publisher disclaim any liability in connection with the use of this book.

All rights reserved. No part of this book may be reproduced or transmitted in any form whatsoever without prior written permission from the author and publisher except in the case of brief quotations embodied in critical articles and reviews.

Contents

Introduction	5
Chapter 1 The One and Only John T. Benson	7
Early Life	7
Designing Zoos	8
Importing Animals	8
Can We Visit?	11
Chapter 2 The Strangest Farm on Earth	15
The Press Notices	15
Transportation to the Farm	18
A Constantly Changing Farm	19
Betsy Arrived and Stayed	19
Building the Farm Into a Park	20
Benson's Reign Ends	23
Chapter 3 Growing Up at Benson's	25
The Lion Trainers	29
A Lion Escapes	30
The Greatest Animal Trainers of All Time	31
Lovejoy Love of Horses Began at Benson's	33
Chapter 4 The Lapham Years	38
Working at Benson's	38
The July 13, 1959 Robbery	45
The 60's	47
A Beloved Gorilla	49
Another Owner Death Leads to a Sale	49
Chapter 5 Joe Arcaris	50
Chapter 6 The Provencher Years	54
Improving the Park	56
The Fountain of Achilles	58
Marketing with Help from the Presidential Election	59
The Elephant Trainer	60
Christmas at Benson's	63
Continued Financial Problems	64

Chapter 7 The End of an Era	**68**
I Always Wanted an Elephant	75
The Years Immediately After the Auction	75
Chapter 8 Where Benson's Used to Be	**78**
State Offers to Purchase Property	78
The State's Offer	79
Circumferential Highway Hits Roadblock	81
Early Property Offers	81
Request for Property for Recreation and a New Police Station	81
Treasure Hunting Requests	82
Animal Conservatory	83
Provencher Disputes Property Value	84
Eminent Domain Taking Completed	85
State Owned Years	86
Establishment of Benson's Historic District	87
Can We Have the Train Depot?	89
Demolition Proposed on the Property	90
New Amusement Park	91
Barn Burns	91
The Future	92
Chapter 9 Benson's Future Secured	**93**
Town Work at Benson's	93
Agreement to Sell	94
Asbestos Lawsuit	95
Park Stabilization	96
Bones Found During Preservation	96
Purchase Price to Go Up	97
Plans for a New Park	98
Bibliography	**101**

Introduction

"Do you know where Benson's used to be?" is the start of many directions given by residents of Hudson. From 1924 until the present and into the future Benson's Wild Animal Farm has been and continues to be a town landmark. Even after it closed for the last time in 1987, the town never forgot.

As this book is being written Benson's is undergoing yet another transformation and will soon become a park in Hudson. While it will no longer be a zoo, the heritage started by John T. Benson lives on and will be preserved by the town and many energetic town volunteers, who have fond memories of this special farm.

For years, New Hampshire had Benson's Animal Farm, the Old Man in the Mountain and Canobie Lake Park as tourist attractions. Today only Canobie remains.

This books looks at some of the unknown and semi-forgotten stories about this wonderful place that enchanted decades of New England families.

And soon the question, "do you know where Benson's used to be?" will become "do you know where Benson's is?".

Chapter 1

The One and Only John T. Benson

John Thomas Benson, born in 1872 in Yorkshire, England, would become known for his animal training, his showmanship and his ability to make money. Benson is credited with putting a sleepy Hudson, New Hampshire on the map. Hudson, a small agricultural town, was changed forever when Benson finally came to town with his animals and his showmanship.

Early Life
Was John T. Benson's father, Thomas, a butcher as some stories cite or was he an animal trainer, and, if the latter, did young John T. Benson learn about animal training at his father's knee? Since history is sketchy from that period, we may never know.

Did Benson perform with his father when he was a young lad as he supposedly told newspapers after he became famous or did he run away and join the Bostock and Wombwell Circus as other stories say? Again, history is sketchy. However, when the Bostock and Wombell Circus traveled to the United States in 1889, Benson definitely came too. After arriving in Boston, he decided to stay. He had found a home. A decade later, in 1899, Benson became a naturalized citizen.

In 1893, Benson married an English lass, Sarah Jane Preston. They lived in Somerville, Massachusetts. In 1896, daughter Marion Alva Benson was born and a second daughter, Edna was born in 1900. By 1920, Benson and his wife had gone separate ways. Although Benson never divorced his wife, he did, later, travel with Miss. E. V. Griffin, his mistress.

Designing Zoos

Carl Hagenbeck, of the German Hagenbeck Brother's Company, took Benson under his wing and trained him to design a more natural habitat for zoo animals. When Benson became their American representative, he designed American zoos, went on safaris to procure animals and trained the animals.

In the late 1895's, Benson designed, built and ran a zoo at Norumbega Park, located at Auburndale-on The Charles River, now part of Waltham, Massachusetts. The park, one of the many recreational areas created by street car companies to increase weekend business, included a 1,200 seat theater, a merry-go-round, picnic and boating facilities, a deer park, a zoo and a restaurant.

In 1911, Benson was asked to be director of the new Franklin Park Zoo in Boston, Massachusetts. A $6 million donation by George Parker made it possible for this zoo to open. Because Benson was by then well-known for his zoo designs and animal training, he was tapped to operate the zoo.

On October 4, 1912, the bear exhibit opened and more than 10,000 people came to see Boston Mayor "Honey Fitz" Fitzgerald release twelve bears into the enclosure.

In 1914 Benson, who had plans for bigger things, left Franklin Park Zoo in the hands of Louis Mowbry, curator of the Aquarium, until a permanent replacement could be hired for Franklin Park Zoo.

Importing Animals

Benson earned a name in the animal import business where he was a very hands-on and talented participant. He traveled on African safaris with many people, including Theodore Roosevelt and William Mann. Mann eventually became Director of the Smithsonian's National Zoological Park in Washington, DC. Roosevelt, as we all know, became President.

In 1914 Benson became the American representative for Hagenbeck Brothers, the largest training company in the world where he would work for the next 30 years. His job was to go on African safaris to select animals to be brought to the Hagenbeck Brother's zoo in Hamburg, Germany. Once there the animals received initial care and training before Benson brought them to America for quarantine and acclimation to the

North American weather. Benson wanted all animals captured and treated as humanely as possible. When he shipped animals, he demanded the best treatment from steamship officials.

Benson housed his animals on a pier on Hoboken, New Jersey, but the animals were actually shipped by steamship to Boston Harbor, and then transported to their destination, or his New Jersey headquarters. His "salesrooms" had a neat oblong side outside that read "Hagenbeck's," but his office had a sign, "Anyone who goes through this door does so at his own risk." Another sign advertised, "Everything in this place is for sale. If you don't see what you want, just ask for it." Benson, always a businessman first, had a golden touch for making money.

In 1918, Benson led an African safari for the Hagenbeck Company. Although he captured a full ship of animals, he was unable to transport them to America because the world was at war. It wasn't until late 1920 that Benson shipped his animals to the Hoboken, New Jersey location.

This was a very large shipment of animals and it wasn't long before area residents objected to the constant smells and sounds. After numerous complaints, Benson was told to take his animals elsewhere. New Jersey was just too populated for his enterprise. Benson knew he needed a more rural setting in which to quarantine and train the animals he acquired

Souvenir Tape Measure
Courtesy of Steve Klein

9

Christmas card from John T. Benson

In 1884 federal laws had been established surrounding animal quarantine requirements and also created the Bureau of Animal Industry whose mission was to monitor and streamline quarantine requirements, track the import and export of animals and ensure the animals were treated humanely. Because Benson took such excellent care of his animals, he never had difficulty with the government over his imports.

Hagenbeck Brothers had purchased the 250-acre Interstate Health Farm in Hudson, New Hampshire for its North American headquarters. This farm had been a tuberculosis health farm at the time of the purchase. Treatment for tuberculosis at that time was to locate patients in a rural, outdoor setting. When Benson bought the farm from Hagenbeck Brothers in 1924, he inherited a few patients. Benson allowed them to stay in their cabins on the farm.

With this purchase, animal transportation ceased to be such a problem. Not only were the animals not being shipped as far, but also the Boston & Maine railroad went through the nearby Hudson Common. Benson decided to have his animals shipped from Germany to Boston and then taken by train to Hudson, which left the animals with only a short trip from train depot to the farm. When his animals were ready for their permanent homes, he could easily ship them via train from Hudson Common to their new destination. The railroad, happy to have the business, worked with him to ensure excellent care of the transported animals.

Souvenir elephant from John T. Benson era.
Courtesy Steve Klein

Can we visit?

This new business immediately drew the attention of local residents who were fascinated with the exotic animals and reptiles moving through their town. Soon Benson was flooded with requests to "look around" his farm.

11

Benson decided to charge admission and hoped that this would discourage the many requests, but he was wrong. People flocked to the farm and enjoyed seeing the ever changing variety of animals.

At some point Benson decided that Hudson residents would not be charged an admission fee. Perhaps he remembered the issues that caused him to leave New Jersey and decided that free admission would make up for the smells and sounds.

Thousands of curious people visited the farm. Benson opened a four acre area where visitors could view the animals. Although dealing with the visitors took time, Benson was still able to train and acquire additional animals. By now he was sending animals to circuses, zoos and even Hollywood for the movies. The Our Gang movies used chimpanzees from Benson.

With every year bringing more visitors, Benson, ever the businessman and showman decided to open The Strangest Farm on Earth.

Courtesy of Hudson Historical Society

Vintage Postcard courtesy of Hudson Historical Society

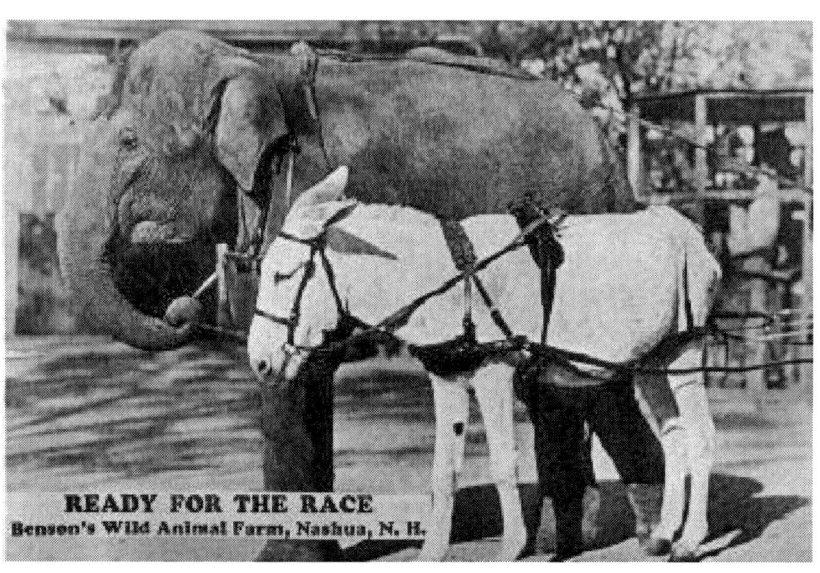

Vintage postcard showing view of lake with merry-go-round in distance.

Courtesy of Hudson Historical Society

Chapter 2

The Strangest Farm On Earth

Benson's attention to detail included the tending to all details surrounding the farm. Not only were the animals exotic, but Benson imported rare plants and flowers, all of which received the same exacting care that his animals received. As a result the farm was very pleasing to visit and the crowds enjoyed both the animals and the fauna.

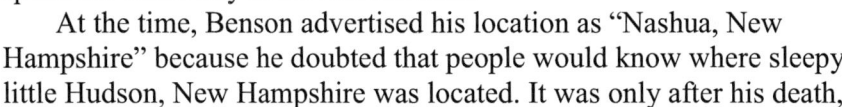

On April 21, 1927 the farm opened its first season as a destination location. In a time before television, there were few other easily reachable attractions, so it was not surprising that families headed to the farm. With all stores closed on Sundays thanks to Blue Laws, Sundays were especially busy. Many visitors brought picnic lunches and planned to spend the entire day at the bucolic farm.

At the time, Benson advertised his location as "Nashua, New Hampshire" because he doubted that people would know where sleepy little Hudson, New Hampshire was located. It was only after his death, when the new owners actually began advertising the location as Hudson, New Hampshire. Nevertheless, Benson brought thousands of people to Hudson during his lifetime.

The Press Notices

When a large shipment of animals from Germany drew the attention of residents

15

in May 1927, the Nashua Telegraph decided to report on the variety of animals arriving in Hudson. These regular reports attracted more visitors and Benson was quick to realize the value of regular newspaper reports. In June 1927, Benson invited Telegraph reporters and staff to the farm where he gave them a tour and talked about his work. The continued newspaper coverage brought ever larger crowds so Benson enlarged the parking lot to handle these growing crowds.

With attendance growing, Benson began to think about other ways to increase revenue for the farm. His first step was to set up concession stands, place lawn swings overlooking the gold fish pond and work to create a welcoming atmosphere where people would stay and return.

At the end of the 1927 season, Benson began construction on two large buildings intended as winter quarters for the animals. Benson decided that he could attract visitors through the fall and winter by building two large buildings where the animals could be seen. He was right.

Every year Benson added more visitor attractions and amenities. He added a large sunken garden, lily pool and promenade as well as developed more a permanent exhibit that housed stuffed animals and wax figures. "Animal Paradise" was a large exhibit for camels, zebras and other grazing animals. Behind a ten foot tall fence, animals roamed free over several acres of land which included a pond. Benson ordered brush removed to enhance the viewing pleasure of the visitors, who then had a full view of the beautiful animals.

Vintage Postcard

Photo courtesy of Bob Lovejoy

Benson's Wild Animal Farm attracted top animal trainers as long as it was open. It offered these men and women a stable life with no traveling. They lived in quarters on the farm, had a housekeeper who also served as cook and prepared three hot meals a day for the trainers.

Elephant trainer Bill Emery joined the staff at Benson's in 1928. Many elephants passed through the farm and needed to be trained before being shipped to their permanent homes. Benson hired Emery to create an elephant school for elephants that would perform in circuses. With training session times carefully coordinated so that visitors could watch Emery work with his animals, training sessions became an immediate favorite and Benson soon realized that he could expand this idea and have other circus acts perform on the farm. It was the first step to making the farm a permanent tourist attraction.

Transportation to the Farm

In 1929 the Nashua Street Railway began to operate service to the Wild Animal Farm every Thursday, Sunday and holiday afternoon. The fare was 15 cents, with children under age 5 riding free. This not only increased revenue for the railway, but it provided an easy way for those without a car to get to Benson's.

Nashua Street Railway had such success that the Boston and Maine Railroad decided to use their model. At that time the Boston and Maine Railroad was having severe financial difficulties and by the early 1930s it needed to improve profits. The plan was to do this by boosting weekend ridership, and so the railroad began a "Jungle Train" to Benson's. Departing Boston on Sunday mornings, it took visitors to Benson's Animal Farm. The ticket to ride the train also included admission to the farm. Benson saw the advantage to having that train succeed and began sending a trainer and animal to meet the train. Some days it would be a chimpanzee or a llama or a camel, but no matter what animal greeted the train, the riders were thrilled.

Promptly at 4:30 p.m. Sunday afternoon, the train whistle blew. Riders knew that they had 30 minutes to board the train for the return trip to Boston.

A Constantly Changing Farm

Once people visited, they continued to return to the farm. The animals were constantly changing because they only stayed during their quarantine period, which gave them time to adjust to the climate. Each animal received some basic training during its stay, because Benson planned to sell them to other zoos or to circuses. He did not acquire animals to keep until 1927 when he became attached to Betsy.

Betsy Arrived and Stayed

In 1927 an Indian elephant named Betsy was brought to the farm. Originally intended to be sold to a circus, she became Benson's pet. Betsy had a gentle soul and could roam among children and adults with no danger. Benson taught her to carry a Hindu saddle so that she could give rides and often allowed her to roam through the park.

Elephant rides began in the fall of 1928. Amazingly that attraction brought in as many visitors as a sunny summer afternoon. People were enchanted with the idea of riding on the back of an elephant and everyone wanted to try it.

Perhaps Benson had a special place in his heart for elephants. Certainly many elephants would come and go through the doors of the park. After Betsy stayed, she became a symbol for the animal farm and her photo appeared on many souvenirs offered for sale in the farm's gift shop.

Benson recognized the elephant's value as an ambassador, using her in various publicity events around the region. This was a change in the farm's purpose and the beginning of a more zoo-like situation. Betsy because the first and perhaps most famous of the animals on display during Benson's years.

Building the Farm into a Park

Benson's Wild Animal Farm was also renowned for providing interesting and strange features as well as changing exhibits. Where else could you see a pig wearing a dress or try to climb a smooth 72 foot pole to capture the ten dollars secured to the top? Chimpanzees were dressed in pants and suits. There was a pig pulling a cart with a sign stating "bringing home the bacon." Benson knew how to increase sales and continued to change attractions, add statues and features. He was also on hand to work the crowd and the people loved that.

Lucky Elephant, a large concrete elephant, was perhaps the world's largest piggy bank. Lucky had a slot in its back and if you could throw a coin in, it was rumored that this would bring you good luck. The money tossed into Lucky Elephant was donated to a variety of charitable causes.

Vintage Postcard of Lucky and the windmill

There was a fortune telling windmill that hid a water tank. Spinning the wheel and learning your fate was a desired pastime. As the wheel was spun, water was pumped and sent to various park locations. Because the visitors loved to spin the wheel, Benson was spared the cost of installing an electric pump to pump water throughout the park. A beautiful Totem Pole exhibit intrigued visitors. Until the park closed there were totem poles on exhibit. Pony and elephant rides were favorites.

Betsy was the most memorable animal. Benson had a set of stairs built. Betsy would walk between them and people would climb up onto the seating secured to her back. She also performed in shows, walked in parades and with her trainer meandered through the farm to the pond where she frolicked in the water while the crowds watched.

Something new was happening every day at the farm. Benson soon realized that people loved to feed the animals and began selling food so that they could. This saved him money while providing more entertainment. That practice is still popular in zoos today.

Benson opened a gift shop and souvenirs became quite popular. Over the years a wide variety of offerings tantalized visitors into leaving some of their money in the gift shops. Miniature brass animals were an immediate hit in the gift shop.

With souvenirs, animal food for sale, admissions and snacks for visitors for sale on the farm, what began as a way to stop the curious became a thriving self-supporting business that gained national renown.

The Circus Fans Association of America held their annual convention in Boston in June 1931 and included a trip to Hudson to visit Benson's Farm. Always the showman, Benson had Betsy standing at the gate with a welcoming sign in her mouth. "Welcome Circus Fans" was their first impression of Benson's. The members dined at Benson's while watching Betsy perform. The had such an enthusiastic response to Betsy's show, that later Benson said their response was what prompted him to add other circus shows to his offerings.

With that decision made, Benson proceeded with his usual enthusiasm and dedication. He realized that expanding the circus aspects would not negatively impact his import business as he owned property that was not being used. Ever the businessman, he saw that this land could be improved to show the circus acts, thus expanding his revenue with increased audiences at the farm.

In April, 1933 Benson announced, through press releases, that he would have a permanent circus at his farm with daily shows. He proudly proclaimed that over 100 animals would be used in the circus shows on a daily basis.

Benson was a local celebrity, who enjoyed people and the community. He often spoke at community events and always had interesting stories about his safaris and his animals. He enjoyed the public attention and was an engaging speaker.

Perhaps his greatest gift was the opportunity to capitalize on any potential money making event. Following the 1938 hurricane, many photos of Betsy clearing damaged trees appeared in newspapers providing free publicity for his growing business. When a bull moose from Canada was on the farm, it was no surprise that Benson invited members of the fraternal Loyal Order of Moose to come and have their pictures taken with the moose. Not to be outdone, the UNH Wildcat football team came each year to have its picture taken with – what else – a wildcat. Benson also worked with the Nashua Lions Club and was known to invite children to the farm and treat them to a day they wouldn't forget. Almost naturally he began summer outings for businesses and organization that came and spent a day at the farm.

John Simo, who visited Benson's as a child and then worked there during the Lapham years, remembers meeting John T. Benson. "He would stand at the entrance to the maze with his dog and chat with everyone. He always had a smile."

Benson was a hands-on owner who also continued to travel extensively. Thanks to his ability to hire capable managers who could run the enterprise during his lengthy absences, he did not have to give up his work for Hagenbeck. From the time the farm opened until 1937, when he finally retired from Hagenbeck, Benson continued to travel on safaris and bring animals back. Finally in 1937 he retired with plans to concentrate on his farm.

Benson's Reign Ends

After only five short years, the farm closed. It was 1942 and World War II was in full swing. Rubber shortages, gas rationing and deplorable economic conditions meant a huge decrease in the number of visitors. Realizing that it was no long profitable to stay open, he closed, but intended to re-open after the war if he could not sell his farm. Neither event happened because John T. Benson died on September 18, 1943 and was buried in Lexington, Massachusetts.

He left an extensive will that showed he had planned for his death. According to the will the Secretary of the Lexington, Massachusetts Masonic Lodge had money to cover his funeral expenses.

Photo courtesy of Hudson Historical Society

His will directed that "my dog and parrot known as "Roger" to be humanely killed at once and to be buried with me…."

Benson had left his mistress, Miss W. V. Griffin, with financial 'notes', which his will directed should be immediately paid. The provision in his will read, "the said Miss E. V. Griffin is entitled to nothing from my estate except the payment of any such notes as a complete settlement of all claims which she might have against me…"

Although his daughter Marion died before him, but Benson remembered her daughter, his granddaughter, in his will and gave her the sum of five hundred dollars. He remembered his wife, his other daughter Edna, Thomas Benson, Senior, Earl Benson, Thomas Benson, Junior and a number of other people.

His books were given to the Hudson library. Betsy, his prized elephant, was given to the Franklin Zoo if they would pay transportation costs, which they refused to do. On November 8, 1971, Betsy died of natural causes and was buried on the farm.

Riding Betsy was a favorite pastime at the farm.

Photo courtesy of Bob Lovejoy

Chapter 3

Growing up at Benson's

Imagine that you are a six year old boy, who lives on a farm filled with zoo animals and circus acts. Would you be thrilled? Bob Lovejoy was. For a decade, he and his mother, Vera, lived at Benson's Animal Farm. It was indeed a dream come true.

Because World War II brought gas rationing and rubber shortages, which led to a sharp decline in attendance at the farm, Benson closed his farm to the public for the duration of the war. It was his plan to reopen after the war ended, but that never happened because Benson died in September, 1943.

On April 8, 1944, new owners purchased Benson's Wild Animal Farm. The Boston Garden Corporation, owned and headed by Raymond W. Lapham, would own the farm for over two decades. Lapham's three co-owners were Walter A. Brown, one time owner of the Boston Celtics, Harry G. Collier and Charles G. Keene. The Boston Garden Corporation

operated the Boston Garden, the Boston Arena and a chain of gas stations when they bought Benson's. Although the four men promised to operate the park as Benson had done and said they had no intention of changing its name, some change was inevitable under new ownership.

When the park reopened, they discontinued the practice of selling animals to circuses and other zoos and, instead, concentrated on running Bensons as a more traditional zoo. Under Lapham, the number of animal species on display increased and the displays became more static as animals no longer came and went as they did under Benson's business plan.

Lapham also purchased the train that ran until Benson's closing in 1987. At first the train ride was short, but because people loved it, additional track was added and soon it chugged by animal displays that you could only see from the train.

At the re-opening Henry Collier managed the farm, but in 1947, Vera Deering Lovejoy earned the title of Farm Manager. She and her six year old son, Bob Lovejoy, moved into a house owned by the farm.

Bob said that he and his mother, his great aunt, Myrtel MacLeod and maternal grandparents, Charles and Isabelle Lovejoy, lived in a home that had been the Brown Farm farmhouse, but was sold to Benson's. Lapham renovated the house for them. There was a barn on the property where Lapham stored the black Jaguar that he drove when he was in town.

"That Jag was the envy of all of my friends. Ray was an absentee owner who came up four or five times a year. He and his attorney would ride the train up from Boston and then use the Jag while in town. That meant that most of the time that Jag just sat in our barn. My friends and I would sit in the seats, pretend we were driving and dream of a future filled with black Jaguars," Bob smiled.

"My mother was a true Renaissance woman – well before her time," said Bob. "She attended Burdett College, established in 1879, was the sole breadwinner for our extended family and still had time to enjoy life. She taught at Burdett College before going to work for Henry Lapham and after Henry died, she went to work for his son, Ray. When Ray bought the farm, we moved to New Hampshire and she soon became farm manager."

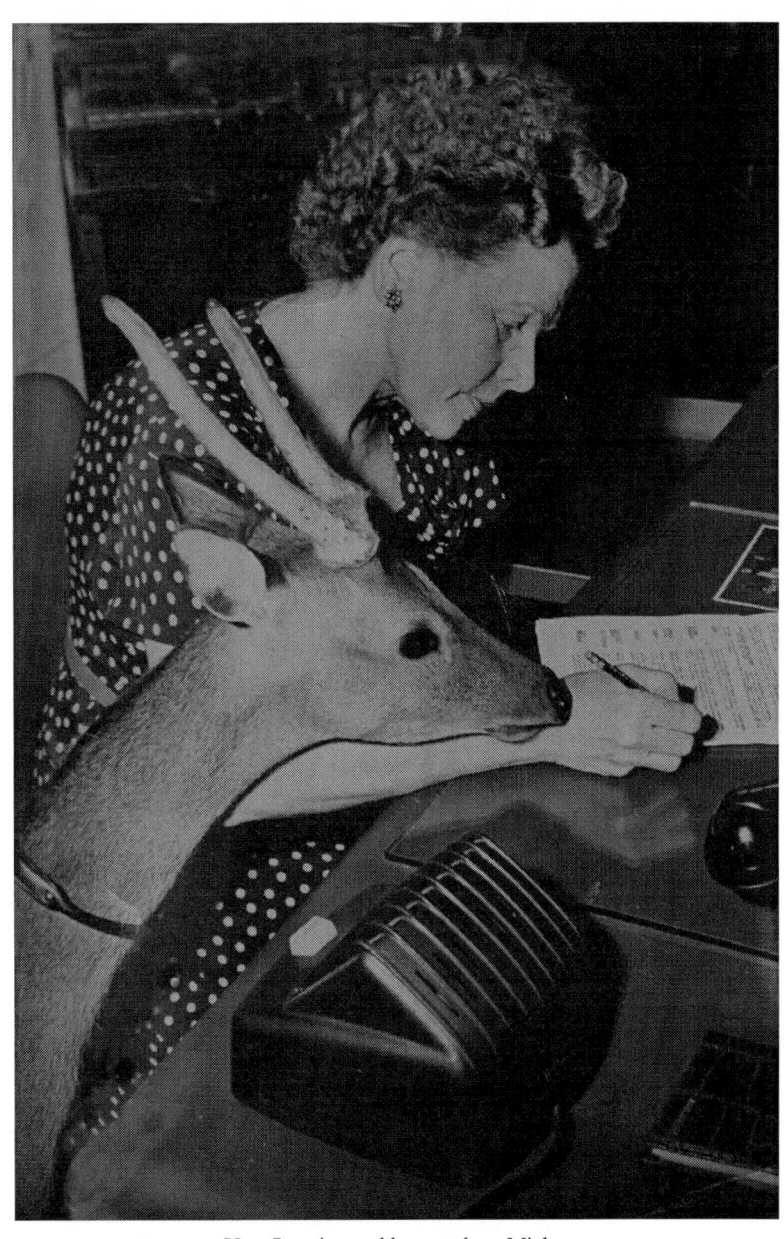

Vera Lovejoy and her pet deer, Micky
Courtesy of Bob Lovejoy

Vera adopted Bob in 1940 as a single mom, which was unusual at that time. "It was rare for the courts to allow that," said Bob, who still has the receipt for $25 that she paid her lawyer to handle the adoption. "She was a great mom. I was an adult before I really understood the responsibilities that she took in when she became the single family provider."

Almost as soon as she began working on the farm, Vera showed a talent for working with animals. "We always had some animal or bird in our house that needed special care," recalled Bob.

For a young boy, it was an enchanted time. They had two cocker spaniels, named Honey and Sandy, who lived in the house with them, but it was the animals from the farm that intrigued Bob.

Vera raised Micky, a Japanese Seka deer, from birth. He needed to be bottle fed so she took him home, much to her son's delight. There she bottle fed him and the deer quickly learned to live in the house.

"I remember that mom got up every two hours to bottle feed Micky when he was an infant," smiled Bob. "That deer was more like a dog than anything else. He followed her everywhere. If we went someplace in the car, he got in the car and rode along – just like a dog."

Vera did the banking for the farm and when she had to go to Nashua to bank, Mickey would go along and would follow her into the bank. "He'd ride in the front seat and then get out and go inside the bank with her," said Bob, who noted that the deer went to work with his mother every morning.

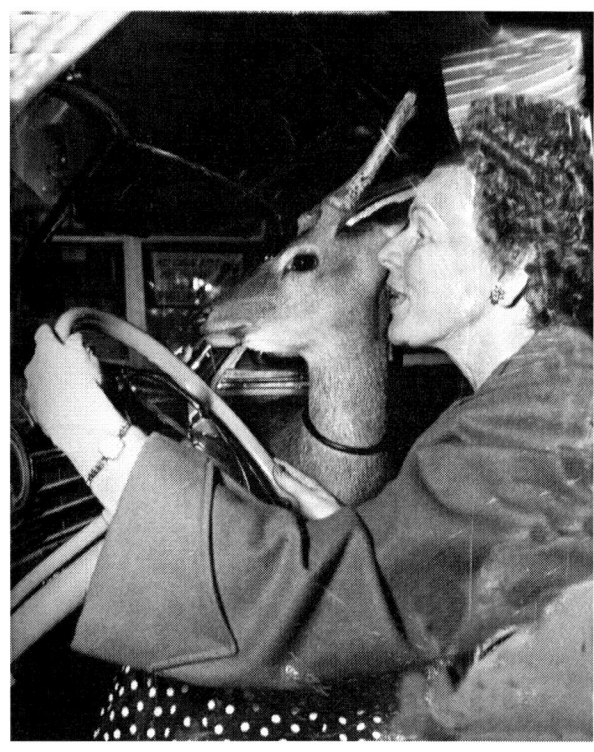

Vera Lovejoy driving in her car with her pet deer, Micky.
Courtesy of Bob Lovejoy

John Ferbert, who worked at Benson's and still lives in Hudson, remembers Vera walking through the park with her deer following her.

Bob Lovejoy remembers a house that always had an extra animal or bird. "We often had birds or animals in the house that my mother would doctor. Many of them couldn't be left alone all night. She always set the alarm clock and got up and tended to them." But sometimes, the animals turned the tables.

Bob talked about one night when he and Vera were awakened by loud bear cubs. Benson's got the bears from Canada every spring. Many times some of them were so young enough they had to be bottle fed. "We had some of them in the house. They slept in a cage, but that one night they woke us up. They had gotten out of their cage and were having a wonderful time climbing curtains. We had to get them down and back into their cages so we could go back to bed."

Bob Lovejoy believes that the bears currently at Clark's Trading Post in northern New Hampshire are still from the line of bears that they acquired from Benson's.

Vera was a valued employee and eventually Ray Lapham made her the general manager for the corporation. "My mother took over all the maintenance and approved all the work done," said Bob.

The Lion Trainers

During the years that young Bob was growing up on the park two of the greatest lion trainers, Josef Karl Walsh from Austria and Joe Arcaris from Glasgow Scotland, of the time were his friends.

Courtesy of Bob Lovejpy

Walsh had studied for years in Europe where he learned from the masters, including the renowned Alfred Court. He trained many lions and tigers for European circuses before joining the British Bertram Mills Circus.

While touring with Bertram Mills, Walsh caught the eye of American circus scouts who began sending glowing reports about his skills back to America. Walsh used no gun and did not take a chair into the ring with him. He was fearless and his shows caught the audience's attention.

When the circus finally toured in America, Walsh liked the new land. At some point he also performed with the Ringling Brothers and Barnum & Bailey Circus before he was offered a position at Benson's and like others, the thought of a stable home was very appealing and he moved in.

At Benson's Walsh worked with both lions and tigers. His show was performed inside an arena with no roof, which was a novelty at the time.

Walsh married the gorgeous Zeaholen, who had been a circus performer. He and his wife, known as Zeak, enjoyed life at the farm with its easy-going pace.

A Lion Escapes

One day Vera made a frantic call home and requested that her son be kept inside. "She didn't want me outside because one of the lions was loose," grinned Bob. One of Walsh's men had left a door open and the lion decided to take a stroll around the park.

"Joe Walsh lived in the old train station which was behind the grange. My mom called him and he came over immediately, looked the lion straight in the eye and slowly walked toward him. The lion backed up until he was back in his cage. The cats had so much respect for Joe that they paid attention to him. Joe called cats by their names and they seemed to know their own names. He was one of the few to work lions and tigers on pedestals at the same time. They obeyed him and listened. I loved to watch him with his cats."

Bob attended Hudson Center School, a 2-room school house with first through fourth graders. When he entered fifth grade, he had to transfer to Webster Kimball School. "I decided I didn't want to go to school anymore, but my mother had different ideas." Vera decided to talk about the problem with Josef Karl Walsh, the lion trainer. After Vera talked to Walsh, Bob got a treat that made him the envy of his school mates. Walsh would pick him up and drive him to school every morning. Suddenly going to school was the thing to do.

Both Walsh and Arcaris were world renowned big cat trainers, but to a little boy, they were just friends who loved big cats. "They both had piercing stares. They used those stares on the big cats and it stopped them in their tracks. If Walsh would call a cat's name and stare, that cat would become motionless."

Esther McGraw also remembers that piercing stare. "Their eyes were frightening when they were getting ready for a show."

"It was time for them to focus," recalled Bob Lovejoy. They needed that icy concentration to keep all those big cats in line.

The Greatest Animal Trainers of the Time

Bob Lovejoy got to meet some of the greatest animal trainers of the time. Doris Archambeault was the bird trainer, but she actually started working in the stands and gift shops. "She was a beautiful girl," recalled Bob. It wasn't long until Harry Collier decided that she should be trained to run the bird act. When appearing with her birds, she wore dresses and heels and often carried a purse. Women in the audience could relate to that because they were wearing hats, dresses, heels and also carrying purses.

Doris would frequently walk through the farm with one of her birds on her shoulder. Children would ooh and ahh and parents would laugh. The beautiful trainer and her birds brought joy to the crowd.

Doris Archambeault.

George Marshall trained the chimps. Fred Pitkin taught Bob Lovejoy to love horses, but his real job was to train the horses and ponies.

Fred Pitkin

German Carl Neuffer was the elephant trainer. Born in 1902, Neuffer learned his craft while working at the Carl Hagenbeck Company. Benson hired him shortly after he opened his business in Hudson because Neuffer was a renewed elephant trainer, whose elephants thrilled the crowds with their repertoire.

Although Bob Lovejoy remembered that Neuffer worked primarily with Betsy, he also worked with others and could make his elephants do amazing tricks from dancing to doing headstands. During a show, he would choose a pretty girl from the audience to ride Betsy. Neuffer would then send the elephant on her way and tell the crowd, "Ok, show's over. Go on home." This always got a laugh and the girl always returned.

Imagine being a young, growing boy and getting to sit and watch your favorite large animal shows over and over.

In later years, Neuffer worked with other animals at the farm. After 30 years as a trainer, he retired from Benson's in 1962 and died in June 1969 after a long illness. He will always be considered one of the best animal men in the business.

"Only when I grew up and looked back did I understand the quality of people working with the animals and birds," Bob Lovejoy said. "It was a magical time for a little boy."

Lovejoy's Love of Horses began at Benson's

Although the farm had discontinued its breeding program, some Shetland ponies were bred up until 1953. Bob remembered the tiny ponies with the sweet temperaments.

Ponies were the dream of all young kids. Bob talked about the pony track behind the old shoe. "Kids lined up to take pony rides." In the summer, kids from summer camps would come to park and all wanted to take a 15 cent pony ride. "It was the highlight of their day," said Bob. Some kids could ride the pony at the old pony track without a leader and others needed to have a staff member lead the pony around the track. Bob's wish is to see a marker commemorating the old pony track placed on its original location when Hudson re-opens the park. Bob was also thrilled with the ponies. He had an unusual opportunity of having his own pony thanks to the arrangements made by Vera. Bob bought a pony from Benson's and kept him at home in the barn. "He was a birthday present. I learned a lot about taking care of animals." Bob said that he and his

Bob Lovejoy and friends.
Courtesy of Bob Lovejoy

friends used to ride the pony. Finally the day came when Bob was grown but the pony was still a pony and he wanted a larger horse. At that time the farm bought him back for fifty silver dollars.

Bob immediately moved on to donkeys. "We kept two donkeys in the barn and my friends and I could continue to ride in the back." That's where one of his friends, Buddy Gordon Moore, began his lifelong love of horses.

Buddy's family owned Moore's store, which is where Cahill's Sub Shop is now. "They lived above the store in an apartment and Buddy and I used to ride together on those donkeys," said Bob. During those years Bob worked at the Moore grocery store rather than on the farm. Buddy, however, became an assistant horse trainer on the farm. Today Buddy lives in Cincinnati and raises mini-horses.

By the time the boys had grown, they discovered that rodeo horses were often brought to the farm at the end of the rodeo season. "The rodeo season actually ended in those days in Boston," said Bob. "Ray still owned the Boston Garden and at the end of the season there were always some horses that were sold. Ray bought them and brought them to Benson's where they lived in a pasture until it was time to butcher them. They became food for the big cats. Benson's had its own butcher."

Bob and his friends used to go down to the pasture and ride the horses that were being sheltered there. "We all just loved to ride."

Harry Collier, who had been in advertising at the Boston Garden, had media contacts. He was responsible for the advertising that pulled in the crowds. Collier and Vera worked together on the publicity.

Collier used his many media contacts, and when Lapham decided he wanted a Liberty Horse act, Collier spread the word. Soon Fred Pitkin, who came from Springfield, Illinois, was hired. He was a good horse trainer and Lapham needed him to work with the palominos they acquired during an animal shopping trip to the Midwest. "Ray wanted horses equally matched and Fred managed that. I remember them as truly beautiful. In a Liberty Horse act, the horses wear head dresses so they needed to be the same size." Buddy Moore was Assistant Trainer. "It was a beautiful act. I loved to watch them."

Many of Bob's memories ar of people who came to the farm and the people who worked on the farm, among them John Ferbert. It was a perfect job for John because he said he loved the animals and loved watching the visitors. Part of his job was watching the barn, guarding it from careless smokers who drifted to near to the wooden structure and the hay that was always on the ground.

Chief Young Thunder Cloud came from Oklahoma and worked at the strangest farm on earth for a couple of seasons. Bob recalled him as a gentle man who also drank like a fish. "I remember the head dress that he made for me." The head dress was an authentic Indian head dress. "He also made a tom tom for me. I took Chief Young Thunder, the head dress and the tom tom to school for show and tell." Chief Young Thunder Cloud entertained the students by talking about his heritage and performing a traditional Indian dance for the students. "Who else has memories like this?" Bob wondered.

Carl Neuffer purchased two baby elephants from Siam, which is now Thailand.

Bob Lovejoy in head dress made by Chief Young Thunder Cloud. *Courtesy of Bob Lovejoy*

"They were shipped with a caretaker / keeper because they couldn't travel alone," said Bob. By the time the baby elephants and their keeper arrived in Hudson, the keeper was very ill. "My mom just brought him home too and he spent two weeks in our upstairs bedroom. She nursed him back to health." During that time, the keeper's visa was going to expire and Vera managed to get it extended until he was well enough to travel.

Finally life on the farm came to an end for Vera and her sixteen year old son. "She felt burnt out in 1953 and went into real estate in Nashua," said Bob. According to her son, Charlie Keene, who was Lapham's attorney, and Vera had some friction she decided it was time for a change and opened her own real estate office.

"Up to her death, she was a woman ahead of her time," smiled Bob. "Not many women owned their own businesses at that time, but that didn't stop my mom from starting what turned out to be a successful business."

Bob graduated from Nashua High School. After time in the Army, he had a successful career in grocery store management. However, his love for horses has been passed to his sons and grandchildren. "My granddaughter was in the Vet Tech program at Alvirne High School, had horses at home and took her favorite horse to college with her."

Bob Lovejoy in 2010

37

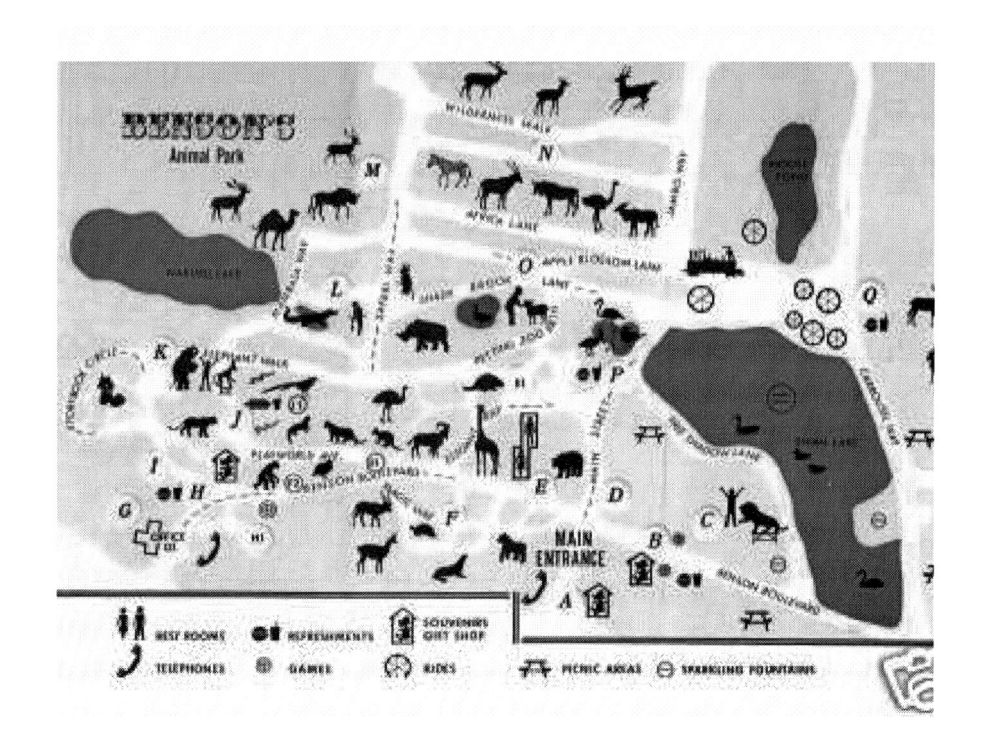

Chapter 4

The Lapham Years

Benson's continued through the fifties and into sixties as a major attraction, but it was beginning to fight with other amusement attractions. Ray Lapham continued to be an absentee owner.

Families continued to flock to the park, including the family of the current New Hampshire Governor, John Lynch. When Lynch attended events in Hudson, he frequently spoke about visiting Benson's as a boy in the fifties and expounded on how magical those trips were. Charlie Keene became the farm manager after Vera left, but life at the farm continued.

Working at Benson's

Mornings began with an early breakfast for staff who liked to share a donut and cup of coffee before the workday began. "We used to arrive before 8:00 a.m. and 9:00 a.m. Louise's Donut Shop in Nashua used to deliver donuts to us. We paid for them, of course," said Lucille Boucher, who has fond memories of eating donuts and drinking coffee with other staff members before the day started.

Ray Lapham
Courtesy Bob Lovejoy

Lucille worked in a refreshment stand by the big cat show ring. "During the week we'd do our own cooking, but it was so busy on the weekends that we'd have grill men who would come in and cook the food for the customers and then we just served." Hot dogs, hamburgers, soda and popcorn were the main items.

Vintage Postcard of the era

    Wages were a whopping $1.20 per hour at that time. Benson's still had a "farm" designation and paid farm wages.
    Lucille laughed about her working attire. "I wore skirts and some days, pants. People did not wear shorts and they didn't wear jeans."
    "We'd know when the lion show was going to end and we'd start cooking a big batch of popcorn." Hot buttered popcorn smell would waft through the air and people exiting the lion show ring would line up. "We'd have long lines – all wanting popcorn and a drink," Lucille remembered.
    Working at Benson's was a family affair for many families. Lucille's brothers Billy and George worked several seasons. "They worked at the pony ring. The kids all loved the pony rides and my brothers would walk the ponies around the rings if the kids were too small to ride by themselves."
    Her aunt, Caroline Ward, was hired as a cook. The animal trainers all lived on the farm and Caroline Ward cooked their meals.
    "I remember the animal trainers. Joe Arcaris was a quiet man who did his job, walked around the park and took care of his animals. We'd see him off and on throughout the day."
    Work requirements were less strict with fewer governmental regulations in these decades. People didn't clock in for a job. Lucille can remember when someone would be sick and her father, George Stevens,

would be called to help with the animals. "He'd feed the elephants and do whatever needed to be done. Things weren't as formal." Lucille's mother had worked at the farm when they ran a beer garden. "Whole families worked there."

One of Lucille's biggest thrills was riding the elephants bareback. "Boy are those bristles on their backs tough," she laughed. She also got to play with the chimps under the watchful eye of their trainer. "It was just a wonderful time."

One of Lucille favorite places was the park maze. "I don't know who designed the maze, but it was filled with twists and turns. People would run in there and try to get lost and that was easy to do." The maze was formed out of shrubs that grew along paths. Once in, you had to keep trying one path after another until you could get out the other end. "You could hear people laughing and talking as they wandered through it. I hope when Benson's opens as a park that someone will re-create a maze."

Lucille, who had graduated from high school, worked during the fall when other staff members departed for school. "They taught me to run the train and I got to give people train rides."

"It's funny, but today if I meet someone and they don't know where Hudson is, I just ask if they know where Benson's used to be and, of course, they do," said Lucille.

John Ferbert with Betsy. *Courtesy of John Ferbert.*

John Ferbert, who worked with the animals at the farm for Benson prior to World War II, returned to Benson's when he came back from World War II. Vera Lovejoy hired him in 1946 and he stayed until 1951. One of his jobs was to take care of the elephants.

Betsy would let him stand in the curl of his trunk and when he called out "Trunk Up" she would lift her trunk so that he could sweep off her back. When he was done, he'd call out "Trunk" and she would lower him to the ground.

Feeding the lions raw chunks of horsemeat was an adventure. Ferbert said you threw the chunk under the bars of the cage, but tried to stay far enough away from the lions that they couldn't grab you.

One day, he was helping a lion trainer get the animals ready for a morning act. Ferbert took one of the smallest lions out, but she was stronger than she looked and got away. She ran toward the house and Ferbert started yelling for people to get out of the way. Disaster was averted and the young lion was soon returned to her cage.

Ferbert remembers making about $60 a week, not bad money for the time, but he had three kids to clothe and feed so he asked if he could come back at night to scrub cages. That netted him another $20 a week, but made a big difference to his growing family.

Vintage Postcard.
Courtesy Steve Klein

Dick Turmel worked at Benson's in the mid-fifties. Although just in his teens, he recalled that he was allowed to care for the bears. "They knew I had a feeling for the animals."

Turmel loved working with the animals and said that he helped with all of them and worked under the guidance of the trainers and keepers. He recalled one embarrassing trip into the bears' cage. "I had my arms full of food and they were hungry. Although they didn't attack me, they did pull on my belt hard enough that my pants slipped down."

Another day, he was working when he heard two female customers ask each other if they could pet the lion. Pet the lion? Turmel knew that no lions should be in a situation where they could be petted. When Turmel turned around Duke, one of the park's fiercest lions, was out of his cage and standing on the grassy lawn.

"We never put Duke into the shows because he was so bad tempered. We quickly got the trainer and people. People were holding ladders sideways to make a human fence while the trainer tried to corral Duke." Turmel paused and shook his head. "That lion started running straight at me. I dropped my ladder and ran. The trainer was barely able to get control of Duke. It was a very close call," he laughed. Like Lucille he recalls his time working on the farm with much happiness.

Pony-go-round, circa 1948.
Courtesy of Bob Lovejoy

Esther McGraw was 8 when she started working at Benson's. She remembers "a gorgeous place" kept up by a professional landscaper. McGraw, like Bob Lovejoy, remembered the ponies. Her job was leading them and their kiddie riders around the ring. "I did that until a pony kicked someone and they had to stop the rides," she said.

Later, McGraw worked in "the cabin," a shelter near the entrance where tickets and souvenirs were sold. "Admission was 35 cents unless you lived in Hudson and then it was free," she said. "Out-of-towners would look through the Hudson phone book for a name and try to use it to get in free."

The merry-go-round had real horses back in those days. McGraw remembers that people would line up to ride one of the horses. "Later they were changed to ponies," she recalled.

John Simo began working at Benson's when he was sixteen. He stayed there from 1947 through 1951. When he started, he had fond memories of his visits as a child and even today, in 2010, has fond memories of working and visiting at this charmed place.

Simo started working in Number 4 food stand for fifty cents an hour and said that the staff's big enjoyment was watching the many visitors who bought orange soda. "For some reason the yellow jackets loved the orange soda and would start flying around the cup and landing on the rim of the cup." He said that it was entertaining to watch the people start to panic and try to figure out how to save their orange soda, but get the bugs away.

Making popcorn used to be done on a gas stove. One day Simo's gas stove burst into flames. He said

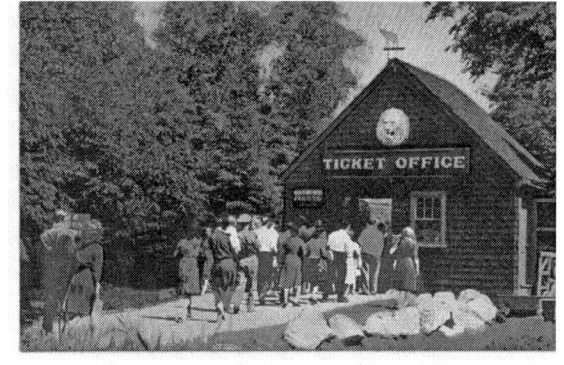

Vintage Postcard. *Courtesy of Steve Klein.*

he remembered that his mother told him to pour salt onto a fire so he grabbed the box of salt and used it to douse the flames.

Working in maintenance increased his pay to 80 cents per hour so Simo switched departments when there was an opening, but working in maintenance was not without its hazards.

One day he was told to wash the windows in the monkey house. There was an 18 inch gap between the wall with the window and the monkey cage. While washing the window, Simo felt his shirt being grabbed. "A monkey had reached through the bar and was tugging on my shirt. I could hear his teeth click together as it tried to get enough material into the shirt to bite. He yanked and yanked and yanked. I finally had to swat his arm to get him to let go."

He also had a close encounter with a lion. When workers needed to work on a pen, animals were moved into another area. Simo said he had

Souvenir lion from Benson era. Note the location of Nashua, NH.
Courtesy of Steve Klein

been told to make some minor repairs in one of the lion's cages and thought that all the animals were safely locked in the adjoining arena. Much to his surprise, the latch on the gate between the cages and the arena had not been secured. While he was working, in walked a large curious lion. "I yelled and backed up and the lion also backed up into the arena. You can believe that I quickly latched that gate."

The July 13, 1959 Robbery

In the dark hours past midnight three men scaled one of the back fences at Benson's Animal Farm and made their way toward the office. They knew that the night watchman, 65 year-old Joseph Pelkey, was making his rounds. Donning grotesque masks, they waited quietly in the dark.

Finally Pelkey returned to the office complex. Entering the kitchen adjacent to the office, he got a glass of water and just as he was taking a drink, the robbers clubbed him on the head. Pelkey screamed and struggled. His face was badly beaten and three teeth were knocked out before the robbers subdued him.

But help was on the way. Lion trainer, Joe Arcaris, who was then 49, lived in an apartment above the office. Hearing Pelkey's screams, he grabbed a baseball bat and stealthily descended the stairs. He hoped to burst through the office door, thinking he would assist Pelkey. Instead he was confronted with a robber holding a gun. Dropping his bat, he put up his hands. Both men were bound with friction tape.

The robbers had come prepared. They tore four phone lines out of the office walls, covered the windows with blankets and then turned on the lights and began to work. Later it was estimated that they were in the office between 2:00 a.m. and 3:00 a.m. Using a blow torch that they had brought with them, they worked on the office safe until they got it open. They took all the cash and coins in the safe and even carried off a pail that contained approximately 50 pounds of pennies that had been collected for the Crotched Mountain Hospital Fund.

It wasn't until 4:30 a.m. that Arcaris managed to free himself and Pelkey. He then alerted Hudson police, who sounded a state wide alert.

Hudson Police Chief Andrew Polak was faced with the third largest robbery ever committed in the state. He called for help from State Police. Before the crime was solved, U.S. Treasury Agents would also be involved.

Arcaris told police that he thought that two of the three robbers had accents.

Ray Lapham and his farm manager, Charles Keene, didn't know exactly how much money had been in the safe. It was the height of the season when the daily revenue typically ranged between $20,000 and $24,000 a day. It was later estimated the amount was close to $23,000.

State Police Sargeant Roger Hilton of Antrim and State Police Lieutenant Carroll Duffee responded. Duffee, the state police fingerprint expert dusted office for prints.

Finally with the help of Treasury Agents Lester Roche, Concord office, and Chester Piskadlo, Lowell Office, plus Lowell Police Lieutenant Victor Koloski and Inspector George Costos, the crime was solved in 1960 and the three men were caught. After the robbery was solved, Polack said that one of the three robbers had been identified almost immediately, but police were unable to gather solid evidence tying him to the crime.

Polack identified three Dracut men, Russell J. Bixby, 41, Everett S. Wancome, 35, and Michael Rodziewicz, 25 as the robbers. All three ultimately served sentences in a federal penitentiary for this plus a score of other crimes, including gun-running. . None of the money was ever recovered.

The 60's

Although the first working television had been demonstrated in 1923, there were few working commercial television stations until much later, but by the 1960s, television and movies were providing a great deal of family entertainment. Benson's was still open, but had declined. Ray Lapham was the only remaining owner of the four man consortium who purchased and re-opened the park after Benson died. Lapham had always been an absentee owner and after Vera Lovejoy moved on, park maintenance was not as much of a priority. During the 1960s and 1970s little money was re-invested in Benson's as Lapham continued to be an absentee owner and the farm showed a steady decline. The animal shows had dwindled to only one per day and attendance dropped and continued to drop.

Souvenir Plate
Courtesy of Steve Klein

But one of the farm's most famous animals would be purchased in 1966. Tony the gorilla came to Benson's and stayed until the auction in the 1980s.

Colossus / Tony in his cage at Benson's

A Beloved Gorilla

Born in the African wilds in the late 1960s, Tony was captured and brought to the United States. In 1968 Benson's Animal Farm purchased Tony for $5,000, but did not display him until 1971.

Gorillas are large and Tony, a Western Lowland silverback gorilla, was no exception. He was 6' 2" tall and weighed over 500 pounds. With little known about gorillas and their life style, it was believed that such large animals should be kept alone so Tony was kept in a large 240-foot cage with inner bars and an outer enclosure, which was built to keep visitors safe.

Tony enjoyed human interaction and became very friendly with his keepers. He loved their attention and responded very positively. He had a sweet tooth and craved sweets and donuts.

It was no surprise that Tony became a major attraction at Benson's. Even those scared of the large gorilla would spend time staring at Tony and his antics. Tony lived in this large cage with a concrete floor. He had no access to the outdoors. As a result, he was probably as interested in the visitors as they were in him. Benson's Wild Animal staff, however, had to be vigilant to ensure that the visitors did not harass the gorilla. But Tony was not as easily stopped. There were numerous reports on Tony's propensity to spit and throw items at the watchers.

Another Owner Death Leads to a Sale.

When Lapham died in 1976, his estate ceased to make any investment in the park and the decline continued. The park continued to operate, but little to no work was done in the park and the park began to show sad signs of aging that were visible to all who attended or drove by.

Chapter 5

Joe Arcaris – The Famous Lion Trainer

    Benson's Animal Farm always attracted renowned animal trainers. One of the draws for the trainers was the chance to live a regular life rather than the nomadic life associated with the circus. Joseph Arcaris was definitely attracted to Benson's for the stable life and freely told people that he disliked the nomadic circus life.
    Arcaris was of Scottish / Italian descent. Born August 1, 1909, in Glasgow, Scotland, son of the late Carmen and Filomena Arcaris, he was educated in Europe. When he came to the United States in 1927, Arcaris tried a number of jobs in his new country before he settled in at Nurembega Park in Newton, Massachusetts where he began to care for the animals. At that time, his dream was to save his money and take flight lessons, but when he learned that pilots didn't have parachutes, he switched to training animals.
    After three years at the Hogo Gardens Zoo in Salt Lake City, learning to train two cougars, he moved to Jungleland in Thousand Oaks, California where he trained animals used in movies. According to his obituary published August 2, 2002 in the *Nashua Telegraph*, "He appeared in several movies, including "Tim Tyler's Luck," a Tarzan movie and an Abbott and Costello movie."
    Arcaris was only five feet three inches tall and weighed 130 pounds. "He was a tiny man," said Esther McGraw, "but boy did he have attention to detail." McGraw, who worked at the farm, recalled one of Arcaris's visits to her home. "After the visit, he sent me two screws and told me to fix my birdhouse. He had noticed that detail just walking up to the house."
    Because of his small stature, every animal that he trained out-weighed him and, frequently, was larger than him, but his height and weight also gave him opportunities to develop unusual acts such as his hand stand on

the backs of his lions. These unusual tricks brought him to the attention of scouts, who were soon singing his praises for his extraordinary and breathtaking feats with his big cats.

Doing the hand stand trick was also a crowd pleaser, but also a danger. Approaching his two male lions from the rear, Arcaris performed a hand stand on their backs. It was a breath-taking and audience pleasing act, but also one fraught with danger. Had he fallen forward, he would have startled his full grown lions with potentially disastrous results.

World War II interrupted his life at Benson's. With Benson's closed, Arcaris joined the Army and fought in the Battle of the Bulge. Although John T. Benson died before his farm could re-open after the war, Arcaris eventually returned to train animals and by the 1950's he had settled in at Benson's where he worked until he retired.

Arcaris lived on the property in an apartment provided to him. He worked year round with the animals. Although he was known for his lion and tiger act, he trained bears, monkeys, elephants, pumas, chimps and the park's 16-foot python.

One of Arcaris' best-known acts at Benson's was a comedy act that involved a marriage ceremony between a lion and lioness.

Arcaris presided over the ceremony. Bobby, the lion, wore a jacket, a necktie, a top hat and spectacles. The lioness, Betty, wore a spotted print dress, necklace, bonnet and glasses. The two lions would look at themselves in mirrors. Bobby would also smoke a pipe and shake Arcaris' hand. After the wedding ceremony the lions would eat a wedding meal.

During the times that Arcaris was in the ring at Benson's, the park was very quiet --- everyone crowded around to watch.

He became known throughout the region for his acts. Unlike other animal trainers he never used a whip during his acts. He entered the cage armed only a buggy whip, but that went unused. In a news story, Arcaris said he loved the animals he worked with like a brother or sister. "I wasn't in love with animals when I started training them, but the longer you're with them, the more you understand them and you come to love them like brothers and sisters. They become your family. You enjoy them that way. I talk to them and worry when they're sick, just as if they were my family." Perhaps this is why he did not need a whip when working with his acts.

Even after he retired in the 1970s, he stayed in the area and was living in Nashua when he died at the age of 93.

After retirement Arcaris stayed active and, like other former workers, maintained his interest in the park. Almost up to his death, he worked with a Hudson committee that was researching the park in hopes of saving it. He also gave away much of his memorabilia from the park to various groups including the town Historical Society.

BENSON'S FAMOUS FROLICKING CHIMPANZEES
SAMMY, JERRY AND JUNIOR

Chapter 6

The Provencher Years

Nashua native Arthur Provencher, who owned an industrial park and truck leasing operation in Merrimack, New Hampshire, had a secret dream of owning and operating a theme park. Provencher, like others in the area, watched the slow decline of Benson's. Driving by the park made many, including Provencher, wince at the decay, but unlike the rest of us, Provencher had the resources to do something about it. He entered into negotiations with Lapham's estate. These negotiations lasted a reported three years. "The guy who was acting as the trustee would have me come up to his home at Lake Winnipesaukee to discuss the purchase. He told me that if word got out that they were thinking of selling the farm, the deal would be off." So Provencher quietly made the trip many times to visit the trustee, but the deal never came together.

Finally, Provencher addressed the "elephant in the room," asking what the price would be to purchase Benson's. He was given a figure and countered with one that was $250,000 less. The deal was made within ten minutes. No written agreement was signed, as the trustee didn't believe it was necessary.

Provencher requested something in writing anyway. "I needed something to take to the bank to get the loan," he explained. The trustee agreed to a written agreement, so long as it was limited to three pages. Provencher's attorney was not pleased but complied with the request. On February 28, 1979 it was announced Provencher had purchased the park.

This was a lifelong dream come true for Provencher. After all who wouldn't want to own a zoo? While it sounded magical, in reality it was hard work. Provencher's pride of ownership was visible everywhere. His vehicle license plate even read "My Zoo".

Provencher secured a loan and invested money into upgrades and maintenance. With the influx of funds, the farm appeared to be doing better. Buildings were fixed, animal enclosures were upgraded and plans were made for expansion. Provencher was under pressure from outside developers to turn the farm into a paved amusement park, but he was determined to preserve the farm as it had originally been conceived by Benson, with its primary focus being the animals. He hired consultants who helped redesign and clean the park. Pat Quinn was brought back as a full time zoologist charged with rebuilding the animal collection and developing educational programming for the park's visitors. Staff worked with the U.S. Department of Interior, who helped with animal conservation, and with the Tufts University School of Veterinary Medicine, who helped with the artificial insemination program.

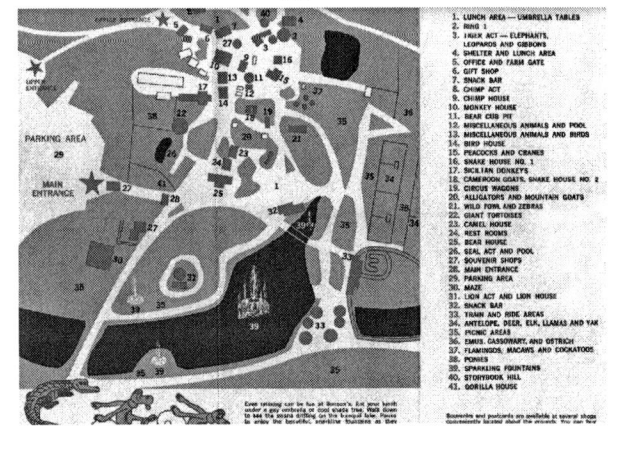

Quinn was appalled at the condition of the park and immediately began working to ensure that Provencher's dream of operating a world class zoo would be realized. Eventually Benson's had more animals than the Stone and Franklin Park zoos combined. Daily performances thrilled visitors and included exotic birds, elephants, seals, and horses. Plus, every season, additional circus acts were booked at the park.

In 1980 a white, female rhinoceros made her first appearance at Benson's. She became an immediate crowd-pleaser and when she gave birth to an 80 pound baby in November, 1981, more people came to visit.

Improving the Park

Provencher hired an in-house artist, Joan Sellers, to create designs for the park—brochures, tickets, drawings and renderings of future expansion. Sellers created new graphic displays with information about the animals that were installed outside the animal corrals.

Provencher closely studied the success of Walt Disney and his theme parks and was determined to turn things around. Visitors were called guests. "Do the right thing" and "make people happy" were Provencher's main philosophies for running the farm. And Provencher himself was seen on the farm almost every day.

As part of his dream Provencher licensed the use of several cartoon characters. With this license, a new show was developed that was aimed at pleasing families and a daily parade was developed.

The parade began at the elephant barn, was led by an elephant often ridden by a beautiful woman. Some days Provencher also would lead the parade, riding the elephant. Behind the parade were cartoon characters and other animals.

Arthur Provencher. *Photo courtesy of Hudson Historical Society.*

Amy Laffin became a character in the parade when she was in fifth grade. For every parade, she and other participants were paid a whopping $2.52. She said they also got a hot dog or drink and were allowed to stay in the park without paying an admission.

Amy and her fellow "characters" had choices of characters. The three little pigs, Foxie Loxie, Mother Goose, Humpty Dumpty, Big Bad Wolf and Little Red Riding Hood, three blind mice and other characters paraded through the park with every parade.

"People lined up along the parade route to watch us. We'd wave and bow. It was so much fun," said Amy.

While it was fun, it was also work. The large fiberglass character heads were put on first and rested on the wearer's shoulders. Then the rest of the costume was added. According to Amy, the costume was what held the large heads on. There was one eye hole and one breathing hole.

Amy became a full time employee when she was twelve years old. Cooking hamburgers and cheeseburgers was her specialty. "It's amazing the responsibility I had at my age. Today's kids cannot have the same experiences because of changes to laws. Back then we were paid like farm workers on a farm. It was, after all, the strangest farm on earth." Now instead of making a total of $2.52 for the parade, Amy began making $2.52 per hour.

Elephants ready for parade.
Courtesy of Steve Klein

When she was 12, she took over the sweet shop. "I worked all my by myself. I was responsible for stocking, selling, keeping the money, making change – everything. It was a terrific amount of responsibility for a thirteen year old and I learned a lot." She stayed there until she was sixteen and got her driver's license. "Then I went to work in a restaurant where I could make more money." Amy graduated from Alvirne High School, but fondly remembers her years at Benson's and works today with the committee of volunteers who are turning Benson's into a park to be enjoyed by future generations.

It was a family affair for the Laffins as Amy's sister Cathy also worked at the farm.

"Cathy always wanted to be an accountant," laughed her father, Curt Laffin, who said that his daughter got her start in finance at Benson's where she counted money from the food stands. "It was a great summer job for the kids, but lots of people started their working careers at Benson's."

Today Cathy has married into the Provencher family and is the New Hampshire State Treasurer.

The Fountain of Achilles

In October, 1981 Provencher announced the arrival of the Fountain of Achilles. This jewel had been commissioned in 1737 for the Chateau of Kittsee, which Paul Anton, Prince Esterhazy. The castle was located at the time in a section of Hungary known as Burgenland, which in 1921 became part of Austria. The massive fountain weighed nearly twenty tons and was made out of the same St. Margaret stone used in the famous St. Stephen Cathedral in Vienna.

The fountain depicted the legendary Achilles, standing in a sea shell while driving his extraordinary horses to the Trojan War. Because the horses were supernatural and immortal, Achilles needed no reins to guide them. On the outside are Balius and Xanthus, the offspring of Podarge and the West wind, Zephyros. Poseidon gave the two horses to King Peleus, who married the Ocean goddess Thetis. Peleus later gave the horses to his son, Achilles, who took them to draw his chariot during the Trojan War. In the center is the horse Pedasus, the Plunger. Thetis, Goddess of the Sea and Achilles mother stand with Achilles.

The Fountain of Achilles. *Photo courtesy of Hudson Historical Society.*

Provencher announced the fountain would be placed at the entrance of Benson's Plaza, giving visitors a spectacular scene as they entered the park. Jay Crowley and his crew were given the gigantic task of precision cutting and transporting the fountain from Sterling Forest Gardens near Tuxedo, New York to Benson's.

Marketing with Help from the Presidential Election

With dwindling attendance, there was constant pressure to develop creative marketing programs to keep the Benson name in the public's eye with the hope of increasing revenue through increased attendance.

One idea developed as the 1980 presidential election drew near. New Hampshire has always had the first in the nation primary. Coupled with candidate registration for the race is a small New Hampshire ceremony held for each person who runs for president. New Hampshire Secretary of State William Gardner has registered between 400 and 500 presidential candidates during his tenure and performs the same ceremony for each.

William Gardner
NH Secretary of State

Some of those candidates come dressed in costumes; some are ordinary folks who know they won't mount a national campaign, but who believe they have something to say. All of them fill out the paperwork, pay the filing fee and have their official registration ceremony. Gardner and his staff treat all candidates with the same level of professionalism and courtesy.

Gardner recalled being in his office when his staff asked him to come to the front office. There, to his surprise, he saw two men and a chimpanzee dressed in a snow white tuxedo. The chimp had papers in his hands.

"I wasn't expecting them. I didn't know what was going on," smiled Gardner. At first he thought that one of the men was filing to run for president, but as the conversation evolved, it became clear that the men were attending the chimp, who, in turn, was the official campaign manager for the Benson's Farm gorilla, Colossus.

When Deputy Secretary of State Bob Ambrose joined the group in the front office, he, like Gardner, couldn't believe his eyes.

To run for president one must be 35 years old and be born in America. "The requirements do not clearly state that only a person can register," said Gardner, who said that he was told that the "candidate" was 35 years human years old in equivalent gorilla years and had been born in the Detroit zoo so he met both requirements.

Gardner was also told that the "candidate" was downstairs in a truck parked next to the state house, but because of the size of his cage, only his campaign manager and the two men had come into file.

The chimp had a set of filing papers in his hand and also had the filing fee. His entourage included a plethora of reporters who were busy snapping pictures of the filing.

Ambrose recalled that the chimp, acting as campaign manager, was one of the best dressed campaign managers ever to grace their offices. "We don't get many campaign managers or candidates in tuxedos," grinned Ambrose. "In fact the chimp may have been the most sane campaign manager we ever met."

This campaign was a unique way for Provencher to garner positive and free publicity for his enterprise. Colossus, was included among serious candidates and presidents on a "presidential primary trading cards" collection authorized by the state library, which Gardner has framed in his office today.

Provencher hoped that people, wanting to meet this unusual presidential candidate, would flock to Benson's when it opened in the spring.

The Elephant Trainer

According to Bronson, there were no amusement rides at Benson's. The attractions were the beautiful, bucolic and peaceful setting and the animals. While the park was open during the warmer seasons, the animals needed to be housed and fed year-round. Provencher made some hires. Among them was Bret Bronson, who was a recent college graduate with a degree in animal science.

Bronson had grown up in northern New Hampshire where his father managed a small zoo. Hired on May 18, 1980, he began work with the antelope and primates.

During his interview Provencher had asked him if he'd ever worked with elephants. Bronson recalled remarking that working with elephants sounded "kinda cool." On July 2, he became the assistant elephant trainer when the prior assistant resigned. Bronson worked with the elephants until he resigned. A year later, in April, 1984 he returned and stayed until well after the park was closed.

Bret Bronson.

Bronson was the ultimate showman according to those who saw him perform. He wore bright red trousers and a golden shirt when performing. His elephants were also adorned with red bridles that matched his trousers.

Provencher, like Benson before him, knew the value of a good publicity stunt and Bronson was frequently tagged to go along with him. In one photo that was reprinted in several newspapers, Bronson was dressed as an Arabian holding a camel.

Bret Bronson holding camel during publicity stunt in Boston.
Photo courtesy of Bret Bronson

During those years he thought of the elephant barn as his second home and calls his years at Benson's a "labor of love". Bronson said that he learned much about handling animals while meeting some really fascinating folks.

"In the spring, we'd be tending the animals, but also working on the buildings in anticipation of opening day," he said. Animals would be having their babies, which required extra care and exhibits were being spruced up. The summer brought all the visitors and the animals liked the extra attention. "By fall we'd be starting to hunker down for the winter months," Bronson said. After the park closed, the employees in the animal section continued to work with the animals and to see to their care. At that time the park had over 600 animals, reptiles and birds. It was a big job.

One winter there was a bad snow storm. "The snow turned to sleet and ice. Roads were covered with ice and it was nearly impossible to drive. Only two of us could reach the park." At the park the nearly 600 animals, reptiles and birds waited patiently for food and fresh water.

Inside the park conditions were also icy. Bronson said that Ted and Dan, the two draft horses were hitched to the wagon that was used for hay rides in the fall. Loading the wagon with food and fresh water, he began making the rounds of the animals. "I was just returning to the barn after feeding the last animal, when the hitching broke. I fell out of the wagon

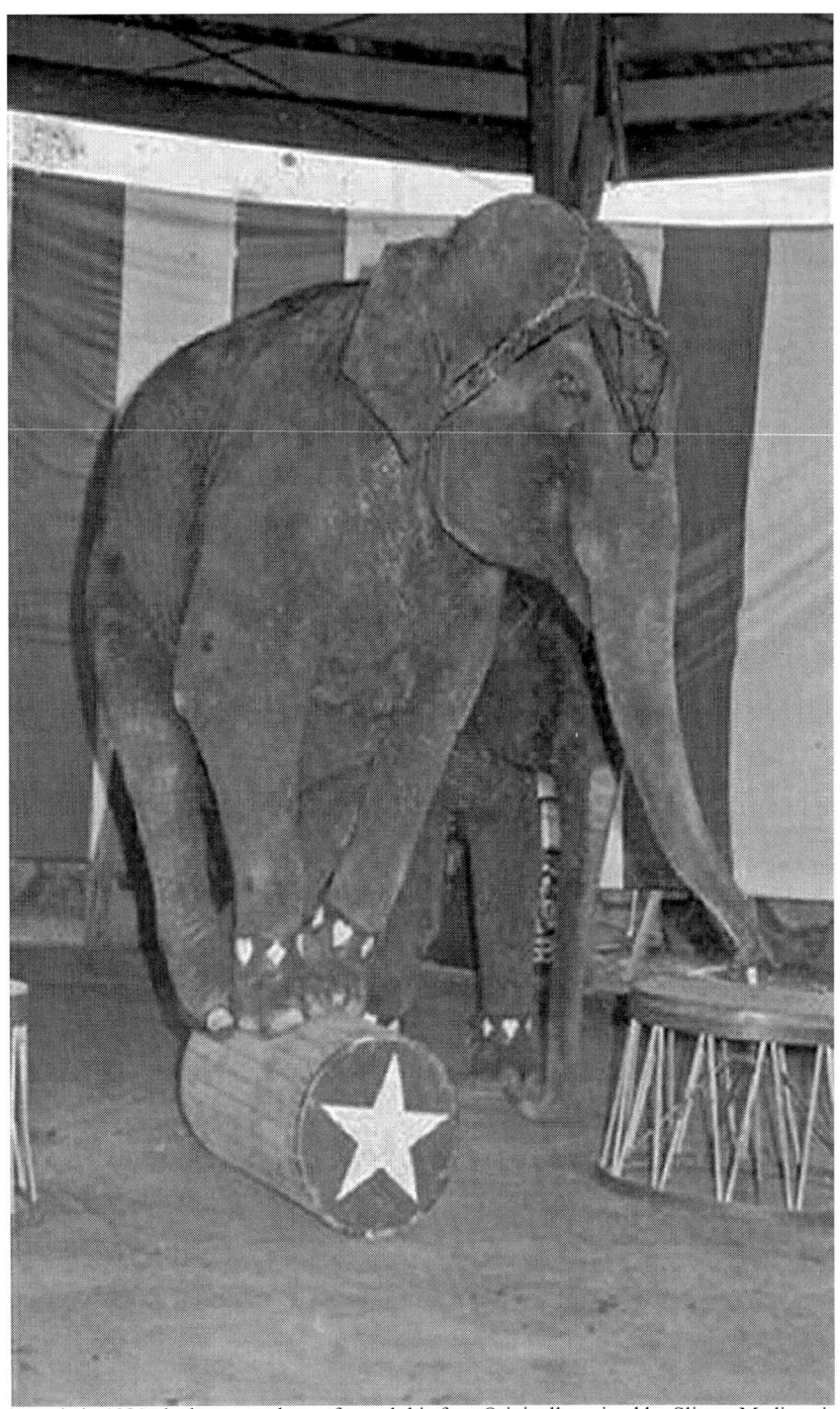

Queenie in 1981, the last year she performed this feat. Originally trained by Slivers Madison in the early '60's, she was one of a small handful of elephants to ever be trained to roll a barrel.

onto my face. My hands were already ice cold. I just took the horses back into the barn and left the wagon for a better day."

Christmas at Benson's

To Provencher's credit, he turned out to be as creative as John T. Benson in his effort to save his zoo. One of his ideas was to offer a beautiful setting to enjoy Christmas. Staff hung thousands of Christmas lights that twinkled in the evening sky during the 1980 and 1981 seasons.

Vintage postcard from 1980. *Courtesy of Steve Klein.*

The well-advertised Christmas display drew in crowds and over 35,000 people walked through winter evenings enjoying the lights. Families enjoyed the stroll through the park, mittens on hands and wonder in their eyes.

The large statues of toy soldiers originally guarded the elephant barn during the Christmas display and are now part of the decorations that Hudson places at Library Park every holiday season.

Despite his best efforts, however, the needed breakeven point was not reached and Provencher announced that he would no longer host a Christmas display after the 1981 holiday season.

Continued Financial Problems
   Despite its initial turnaround when Provencher bought the park, Benson's continued to decline during the 1980s. The cost of housing and caring for the animals was too great. It cost $1,000 a day just to feed the animals. Insurance costs kept skyrocketing. In 1979, liability insurance cost $25,000 a year, but by the time the park closed in 1987, the cost was running closer to $350,000 annually. That amounted to almost $2 per visitor just for liability insurance, but Provencher didn't want to raise admission prices because he wanted the park to be affordable to families.

Souvenir bookmark original printed in color.
Courtesy of Steve Klein

   Although park attendance had increased greatly over 1978 levels, so had costs. It was an on-going battle to try to break even and cover all expenses. A battle that Provencher was not winning despite his innovative ideas.
   One of the on-going problems was the lack of bank financing. Banks saw all amusement parks as poor investments and wanted only to loan money on a year to year basis at very high interest rates. As a result, Provencher tried to reach partnerships with a variety of other amusement organizations.
   Provencher had serious talks with Hersey Entertainment and Resort Company, but nothing materialized. He tried again in early 1984 when he sold two-thirds of the park's stock to Riverside Park, in Agawam, Massachusetts. That joint ownership also failed because of conflicting views of the future and by the end of 1984, Provencher

again had full control. Indian Head Bank claimed the assets, but Provencher was able to re-negotiate his loan and open the park for yet another season.

In 1985, Provencher filed Chapter 11 bankruptcy. At that point he reportedly had a $2.4 million debt with Indian Head Bank and another $1.1 million to other creditors. The future looked bleak.

Nevertheless, a bankruptcy judge approved his repayment plan and the park opened in 1985. Provencher was able to sell 60 acres of unused land to Bay Group, Boston, Massachusetts, for $2.5 million which was used to pay off Indian Head Bank.

A final effort was made to save the park. In its final season, Benson's morphed into New England Playworld and Zoo. It featured amusement rides and included a huge statue of Mighty Mouse. Were the purchases of the amusement rides, which included the Fire Fly roller coaster, Magic Balloon ride, Tilt-A-Whirl, pirate ride, Ferris wheel and others the straw that finally broke the camel's back or was there just no way to save the park?

Inside Playworld brochure. *Courtesy of Steve Klein*

Although Provencher remained optimistic right up to the end, no magic elixir arrived to save the park. This was the last season for the park and zoo, and it closed for good at the end of the 1987 season. A few of the elephants remained for another year or so, but the Strangest Farm in the World was no more.

Closing Ad that ran in the Manchester Union Leader.

Ad courtesy of Hudson Historical Society.

Chapter 7

The End of an Era

Despite Provencher's on-going efforts and optimism, by the middle 1980s the financial future was bleak. For years Hudson had been defined by Benson's and it was a beloved landmark. So it wasn't a surprise that once the park's situation became public many residents joined a petition drive asking the state to take action to keep the park open as a state park, but that effort failed.

Until the very end Provencher worked to keep the park open, but it was not to be. Rising costs, bad press associated with Provencher's financial troubles and an economy that now had more choices for entertainment, all took a toll. Provencher said that the park was in a spiral of always having to provide new exciting attractions while competing for shrinking family dollars in a world that provided more choices and opportunities. Park employee wages were higher and liability insurance premiums were escalating upwards.

Souvenir Patches

Despite the fact that attendance was above 300,000 each of the last two years, the park was losing money. In a last ditch effort, Provencher changed the name to New England Playworld, signed a license to use Mighty Mouse, Deputy Dawg and other Terry Toons cartoon characters as

68

well as spending more than $500,000 on new rides, amusements and landscaping. At the time, the park was the only privately owned zoo in America and Provencher wanted to do all he could to keep it open. Provencher left no stone unturned in an attempt to save his beloved park.

Norman Roberge, who was the park's accountant, announced the park lost more than a million in 1987, its last year of operation. Those losses were equally split between operating losses and capital investment losses. In fact the park had not shown a profit since 1982 when more than 370,000 visitors enjoyed the park.

When the park closed, 44 full-time employees and 200 seasonal jobs were lost. The closure had a tremendously negative impact on employees and residents of Hudson and the surrounding area. An auction was scheduled.

Employees were devastated. Kevin Bosselait, ride supervisor at the time of the closing, said he'd been coming to the park since he was a kid and then started working at the park.

State Senator Rhona Charbonneau tried to develop a plan that would allow the state to preserve the park. She filed legislation asking for a feasibility study on assisting Benson's and urged that her bill be modified to include some kind of financial package. However, it was too late to save Benson's.

Barney, the Trained Macaw, Greets You at the Farm Gate

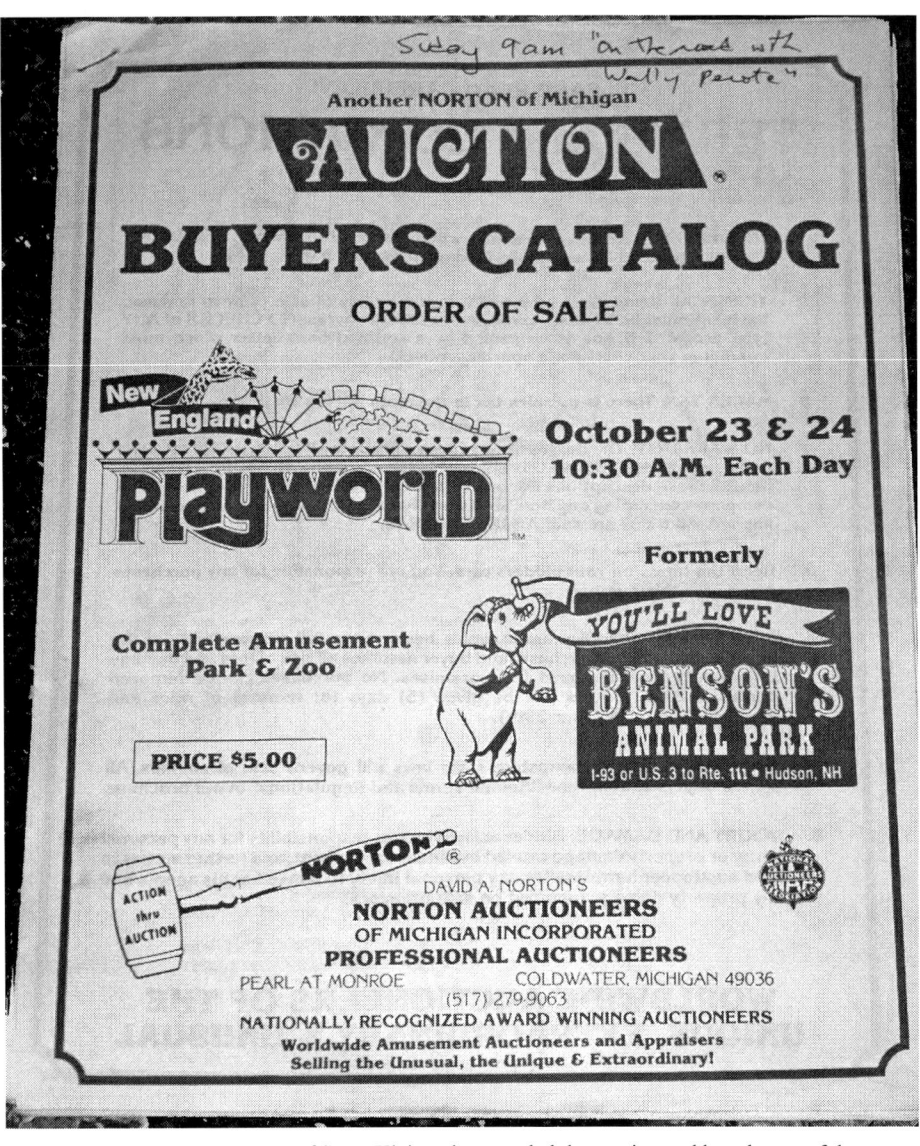

Auction brochure front courtesy of Steve Klein, who attended the auction and bought one of the totem poles which he is restoring.

On Friday and Saturday, October 23rd and 24th, 1987 the auction was held. David A. Norton, president of Norton Auctioneers of Michigan, conducted the auction which began promptly at 10:30 a.m. each morning. Norton came dressed as a carnival barker in a red sports coat and electric blue pants.

Animals, carnival rides, vehicles, attractions, birds, appliances, costumes, reptiles, antiques, buildings and other memorabilia were slated to go – no item was too small.

Attendees were presented with a 46 page listing of items. It was a cash sale with no warranty given on any item. Bidders who wanted to present a check also had to present a certified bank letter which guaranteed the check for a specific amount. To bid at the auction, you had to be a registered buyer. Registration began at the offices of Norton Auctioneers on October 22.

Auctioneer David Norton offered goods. *Photo courtesy of Hudson Historical Society.*

To bid on an exotic animal, small mammals, primates or endangered animals, bidders had to provide the appropriate permits from the US Fish and Wildlife Service. No permit was needed for a domestic animal. Bidders were told the animals would be sold without cages, but with a health certificate. If an animal could not be removed by noon on October 29, the new owner was charged $5.00 per day for feed and care.

Representatives of the Humane Society were on hand to ensure the safety of the animals. The Society monitored sales of endangered species so it could track buyers and animals.

To assist with shipping, representatives from qualified animal shipping companies were on-site during the auction and their fees were paid by the new owners. In addition the park veterinarian would assist the new owners for a fee.

Everyone who attended the auction had to pay a $10 entrance fee. According to the auction company, this entrance fee would keep the auction limited to serious buyers, but still more than 1,200 people attended the first day. People came from Puerto Rico, California and Asia. The San Diego Zoo sent a contingency. Representatives from the Boston Museum of Science, York Animal Kingdom in Maine and the Magic Forest in Lake George, N.Y. rubbed shoulders with those who remembered and paid their entrance fee to see the end.

Steve Klein, who registered and attended, recalls the crowd and said he had been surprised by the amount of interest. Attendees came from all over – some from other amusement parks, looking for a deal and others from nearby who just wanted to have a piece of Benson's to remember.

First on the list was a "big, male ostrich" followed by a "small, male ostrich." The auction brochure noted which animals were captive born, and their lineage if born at the park. After 54 animals were sold, the auction moved into lots of picket fence, fence posts and cages before moving into pairs of peafowl.

The auction, organized by building / area, required walking from place to place. The second area was the elephant barn where reptiles as well as the elephants had been staged. The wood sign for the elephant barn was lot item 163.

Lot by lot the park was sold. It must have been horrible not only for Arthur Provencher, but also for others who loved Bensons to watch the park dismantled piece by piece. Bob Lovejoy said that he attended the auction. "It was the last time I was at the park until this past October's [2009] open house. It was really sad to see all the animals and all the memories being sold to the highest bidder. Saw a lot of previous employees there also and most had a look of disbelief on their faces."

Hawthorne Corporation, a company that provided animal

acts for Shrine Circuses and other indoor circuses across America, bought a complete elephant act, which consisted of Liz, Queen and Jackie II, for $65,000.

Elephant trainer Bret Bronson said that representatives of the San Diego Wild Animal Park attended the auction and had planned to bid on the elephants until they received a phone call from their accrediting society telling them that they would lose their accreditation if they bought animals at an auction. "The society didn't want to see exotic animals sold at auction because they thought it set a bad precedent," said Bronson, "but those elephants would have been better off to have gone to San Diego."

The youngest elephant, Tanya, was an African who had been trained by Bret Bronson. Al Jones of Hanover, N.H. bought her for $14,000.

Benson's famous gorilla, Colossus, was lot 208 and described as a "lowland gorilla – 20 years old, 550 pounds, viable semen, endangered." Quinn wanted Colossus, but couldn't attend the auction so he arranged for Pelham resident Prentice Robinson to attend the auction and bid on Colossus. When the bidding was done, Colossus was sold for $37,000 to the Gulf Breeze Zoo, owned by former Benson Zoologist Pat Quinn. Located in Pensacola, Florida, Colossus would be reunited with Quinn, who provided him with an outdoor area. It had been years since Colossus had walked on grass and been out of a cage.

By the end of the auction more than 500 reptiles, animals and birds had been sold for an estimated $250,000. Bidders with money were able to negotiate some excellent deals. Santa's Village in Jefferson, N.H. bought the park's roller coaster for $197,500. The roller coaster had been purchased and installed at Bensons in 1981 for a cost of $600,000. The Galleon ride reportedly cost $250,000 when it was installed in 1987 and sold at auction that same year for only $100,000.

All of the displays associated with Benson's annual Christmas display also went under the auctioneer's gavel. The wooden soldiers that adorn Library Park in Hudson every Christmas season were sold for $300. Klein recalled that the nativity scene sold for $500 and Santa's helpers sold for $500.

Vintage Christmas postcard.
Courtesy Steve Klein.

Steve Klein, who now runs Benson's Animal Farm Message board at http://www.bensonsanimalfarm.com/, wanted to buy memories. "I was surprised at the amounts that some items were sold for," he said. "I would have liked to have purchased more, but …." However, he did not walk away empty handed. Klein bought one of the famous totem poles. For a number of years he had it sitting in his yard, but decided to restore it and it is now laid out in his garage where he is very carefully removing the added layers of paint.

When the auction was over, Provencher still retained the land. He kept 3 llamas and planned to breed and sell their off-spring. Bronson also kept his animals on the park. According to Bob Goldsack, Provencher retained the 80 acre core of the park plus 140 surrounding acres at the end of the auction. He restarted his trailer rental business at the site and ran it there until he vacated the site at the end of 1997.

I Always Wanted an Elephant

That's how Al Jones, who purchased Tanya, began his recollections of the auction. Jones grew up in West Lebanon, New Hampshire. Almost every season he was thrilled when his parents took him to Benson's Wild Animal Farm. "We usually went twice a year. It was magical to a young boy."

When Jones was five, he was inside the elephant barn. "At that time the elephants were on one side and on the other side were large cages for the big cats. My parents were looking at them. Even then I loved elephants and wanted one." The tiny boy slipped under the chain fencing and ran over to Betsy.

"When my mother turned around and saw me she started screaming. I was happily hugging Betsy and had my arms wrapped around her leg. I guess you could say I just have an elephant problem," he grinned. Both his mother and the elephant trainer were very upset and to this day Jones recalls the very severe scolding that he got.

"I still wanted an elephant. At the time of the auction I was working full time, didn't have a clue how to care and feed and elephant," said Jones. Nevertheless he got a permit and went to the auction. He got his elephant and then realized that he didn't know where he'd keep her or how to feed her. However, he saw Bret Bronson and decided to offer to buy him a cup of coffee.

Before the day was over, Jones and Bronson joined forces. "I hired him to train and care for Tanya," said Jones. "What a relief." Then Jones worked out a deal so that the elephants could stay at Benson's.

The years immediately after the auction

Bronson remained at the park after the auction as a paid employee. It was his responsibility to care for the remaining animals. In addition, he and Jones housed first Tanya and then the other elephants that they acquired in the elephant barn.

While Bronson was caring for the animals, Jones embarked on saving Benson's for Hudson. He worked with Hudson's Town Council. "I thought that Tanya would be the first animal in the zoo, but that wasn't to be."

Jones was brokering a deal with a bank and a developer. The developer would build some condos on the edge of the large Benson property, get a tax credit for opening the zoo and the bank would provide the funding. "Then New Hampshire banks began to fail as the real estate market fell apart. The bank backed out and that was the end of that dream." In the meantime Bronson was still caring for the elephant and llamas housed at the closed park

The first year after the park closed was very strange," Bronson stated. Spring came and went with no opening. Bronson recalled walking around a park that should have been filled with people, but was only filled with silence. Animals sold at the auction were slowly transitioned to new owners until finally it was only Bronson and the elephants and Provencher's llamas.

"We acquired three more elephants in 1990 from a situation where they had been abused. We were on the property until 1995 and then moved to the Southwick Zoo in Massachusetts," said Bronson.

For the years that Bronson and his elephants remained on the property, they would walk down to the pond so that the elephants could frolic in the water. Bronson said he watched some things grow and other things fall down as the verdant New England foliage began to over-grow paths and buildings.

The years between the closing and his move to Southwick Zoo, Bronson, Jones and the elephants traveled around. Bronson developed both an educational and an entertainment package. "We did parades, TV, movies, went to other zoos and fairs."

Jones recalled one weekend when they had the elephants on stage. "I came out and cleaned up if the elephants left a mess," said Jones. Bret was putting the elephants through their paces, but Jones said that they had apparently eaten something that didn't agree with them. Jones made so many trips onto the stage to clean up that he got applause. "It was really embarrassing." Jones said it had been a privilege to work with Bret, whom he called an excellent trainer.

Ultimately Jones took his elephants home to Weare, New Hampshire. "We had room. At the time there were four elephants. We also adopted a lion – Lisa the lion. She would lay on the floor with my kids and watch television with them."

Jones said that his neighbors were not thrilled with his animals and lawsuits ensued. Finally, after a two year battle, he lost in District Court. "My wife and I were talking about taking the suit to the Supreme Court, but then we decided to find homes for the animals. It took us a year. Having exotic animals means someone always has to stay home and we thought we'd like to travel so we decided not to continue the court case and to find good homes for our animals." Even today Jones talks about the fun of living with a lion and four elephants. "Our kids have wonderful memories."

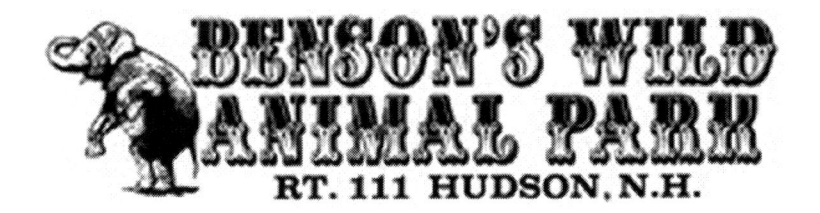

BENSON'S WILD ANIMAL PARK
RT. 111 HUDSON, N.H.

Chapter 8

Where Benson's Used to Be

State Offers to Purchase Property

New Hampshire planned to build a circumferential highway around the Nashua/Hudson / Litchfield metro area. During property acquisition, permitting, and plan development, affected wetlands were identified. New Hampshire Department of Transportation [NHDOT] need to find 38 acres that could be devoted to wetland mitigation. It was no surprise that the Benson property caught their eye.

The former Benson Park location was ideal. It abutted the proposed circumferential. There was plenty of acreage to cover any mitigation plan and it wasn't currently being used. Two appraisals were ordered. The state chose not to use local appraisal companies and this would turn out to be in error, which would result in a lawsuit.

The Benson property was now 165.8 acres situated on an odd-shaped lot that had 900 feet of frontage along Route 111, a central Hudson road. In addition there is approximately 2,100 feet of frontage along Kimball Hill Road and 2,000 feet of frontage along Bush Hill Road. There were a number of buildings on the property, some of which were ultimately designated the Benson Historic District, a connecting system of asphalt pathways and driveways, some asphalt parking, a large grass area, a large amount of mixed hard and softwoods, a pond, plus swamps and other wetland areas. Utilities were located on the premises. The overall topography is level to hilly with some steep areas.

One appraisal, conducted by Leland E. Buzzel of Portland, Maine, indicated that the best use of the property was for residential usage. The appraisal looked at the buildings and other improvements that had been made on the site and deemed them of no value. Comparing four other large residential developments in the area, it was decided that the value of the land was at $6,500 per acre, but it was noted that there were some wetlands that would not be suitable for residential construction.

The other appraisal was done by Leon E. Martineau, Jr. of Thompson Appraisal Company, Inc., located in Concord, New Hampshire. This appraisal reported the property had split usage – some commercial and some residential. It also noted the wetlands issue. A value of $375,000 was given on the 20 acres along Route 111 for future commercial usage. This was based on comparison sales at the time. Of the remaining 145.8 acres, this appraisal urged residential usage and used two local comparison values. They looked at the 56 acres along Kimball Hill and Bush Hill Roads, which sold for $7,500 per acre or $420,000. The second comparison was done for the 90 acres west of the wetlands, which were valued at $3,000 per acre or $270,000. For the total property it was estimated that $1,065,000 was a fair market value.

Based on these estimates Governor Judd Gregg developed a plan that would authorize payment of up to $1,075,000 from the Turnpike Expansion Account for the purchase of the Benson property. NHDOT was authorized to begin negotiations, but was told any contract would be subject to Governor and Executive Council approval.

The State's Offer

On June 19, 1992 a letter was sent to Arthur Provencher for the purchase of the property. The offer letter, written by Carol A. Murray, Administrator, Bureau of Right-of-Way, NHDOT, said, "Please consider this official notification that a portion of your property located Southerly of Central Street, or Route 111, as now traveled, and Westerly of Kimball Hill Road as now traveled, in the Town of Hudson, County of Hillsborough, State of New Hampshire, will be required for the Wetland Mitigation for the Nashua - Hudson #10644 Circumferential Highway, ..." The letter offered payment for damages. "The total amount of damages herein offered is one million seventy-five thousand ($1,075,000.00) dollars and is based on an appraisal of your property and made in conformance with State laws, rules and regulation."

It wasn't really an offer to purchase, as the letter stated, "Under the Statutes, you have ten (10) days to consider this offer. If, at the end of this period you have not indicated acceptance, the Department will initiate eminent domain proceedings under the provisions of RSA498-A, as amended."

Copies of the Murray letter were sent to National Surface Cleaning, Inc., First NH Bank, Town of Hudson, Joseph Bertolotti, Diane Bertolotti, Samuel Racer, Irene Racer, Fox Realty Trust and Gertraud Roberge, all of whom had liens against the property.

By June 25, 1992 Administrator Murray was writing letters with checks to the lien holders to clear the liens, a requirement of the eminent domain taking.

Word of the offer spread and on June 30, 1992 Kevin Landrigan, who wrote for the *Nashua Telegraph,* filed a Freedom of Information Act request that asked for access to any and all documents related to the Benson's property.

On July 14, 1992 NHDOT Administrator Carol A. Murray wrote back that he could review the file. It wasn't long until articles began appearing in local newspapers.

Asbestos

Throughout the years several pieces of property in Hudson have been found to be contaminated by long ago dumping of asbestos. On December 29, 1992 Richard Reed, Supervisor New Hampshire Department of Environmental Services [NHDES] wrote to Administrator Murray that test pits had been dug on the Benson property and asbestos had been found. NHDOT was ordered to take action to remove all the asbestos.

As a result of this finding, work was delayed on the plans for wetland mitigation as NHDOT planners worked on the removal issue. This work stoppage came at a poor time as NHDOT was still struggling to get permits.

Unfortunately, this would not be the last time that asbestos would be a problem on the property.

Asbestos would continue to haunt the property and would, in later years, hold up the sale of the property to Hudson.

Circumferential Highway Hits Roadblock

Originally conceived in the 1950s, this project was fraught with obstacles. By 1992 the state thought they had resolved most of those and moved forward with the Eminent Domain taking of the Benson property, but in 1993 the US Environmental Protection Agency filed an "intent to veto" because of concerns about impacts to wetlands and wildlife habitat in the Southern Segment between NH3-A and NH 111 in Hudson, stating that area of Hudson contains one of the three remaining forest blocks greater than 500 acres in the NRPC region.

With this set back the state began to work on a partial build of the circumferential highway and decided to proceed with the Eminent Domain taking as they still needed to mitigate wetlands. Work on evaluating the Benson property continued while plans for a partial build were finalized. One of the items that needed to be determined was the value of the buildings still on the park property.

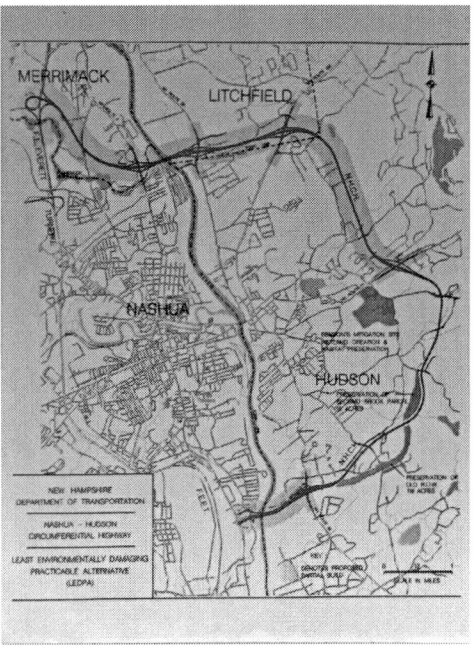

Plan for Circumferential Highway Project.

Early Property Offers

Even before the state acquired the property through eminent domain, others began to ask to buy or use some of the land. Within a few months in 1993, three diverse offers were made to the state.

Request for Property for Recreation and a New Police Station

Growth in Hudson was affecting the town. Hudson Board of Selectmen Chairman Ralph Scott wrote to the state on March 3, 1993 inquiring about the purchase of some of the property for municipal buildings and recreation. Scott wrote that Hudson wanted to purchase thirty acres and would place a new 14,400 square foot police station on a 4 acre parcel and keep the rest for recreational activities. According to Scott,

Hudson had already invested $7,700 in an evaluation and potential design for the police station on this site. Because there would be a town meeting and vote in ten days, Scott was requesting a quick response.

Hudson State Representative Leonard Smith also wrote a letter urging the sale and asking for a response prior to the March 13 town meeting.

On March 12, 1993 NHDOT Commissioner Peter J. O'Leary wrote letters to both Smith and Scott – each was a polite refusal to make a decision at this time. The nearly identical letters said that NHDOT must develop a wetlands mitigation plan and then develop a long range plan for the property. Once those two plans were in place, they would go to CORD (Council of Resource Development), who would have to consider the Hudson request for the recreational usage property. If CORD approved, then the land could be conveyed to Hudson at current appraised value. O'Leary also said, "Should the Circumferential Highway not be constructed, I expect the Town will be extended an opportunity to acquire some or all of the property." O'Leary finished both letters by saying that he understood the urgency.

Because the circumferential highway project had been moving at a snail's pace, selectmen were discouraged by O'Leary's letters. News broke in October, 1993 that Hudson had purchased the 56 acre Unicorn Park Industrial Subdivision for $400,000 or less than half the land's assessed value. A $1.5 million dollar police station approved by voters at the March 13, 1993 town meeting would be built on this property.

Treasure Hunting Requests

The Granite State Treasure Hunter's Club thought the Benson property would make an ideal location for their group's outings and requested permission to hold events on the property. On May 3, 1993 Mark Richardson, NHDOT, wrote to Senior Assistant Attorney General Michael J. Wells stating, "This bureau was contacted last fall by Ron Pinard of the Granite State Treasure Hunter's Club. Mr. Pinard was seeking permissions from the department to allow the club to sponsor an outing at the former Provencher property."

The Granite State Treasure Hunters Club for Historic Preservation, the oldest registered club of its kind in New Hampshire, was formed in May 1974 by Don and Paulette Wilson and was dedicated to the metal detecting hobby with the purpose to promote treasure hunting through safe and responsible practices in the use of metal detecting and recreational gold panning equipment.

Hopes for treasure hunting events were dashed on August 8, 1993 when NHDOT Administrator Murray wrote to Mr. Pinard, declining to allow the club to hold events because the club did not have liability insurance.

Animal Conservatory

The last request made during 1993 for use of the Benson property was made by Curious Creatures, The Conservatory, located in Beverly, Massachusetts. Louis J. Karlberg III, Business Development Manager wrote to the state about preserving the site. According to his letter, Curious Creatures had been developing a plan for an animal conservatory.

Karlberg noted that the organization knew that 38 acres would be reclaimed for wetlands mitigation, but said they were only interested in rest of property. Their plan was to promote, protect and propagate animals. As part of their proposal, they offered to restore all buildings, maintain the park and buildings. To pay for the on-going support of such an animal conservatory, they proposed to open a full-time veterinary clinic that would be open to the public as well as care for the animals living in the conservatory. The conservatory would also be open to the public and offer programming on animals and land and wetlands preservation. When fully

Vintage Postcard from Benson's Wild Animal Farm.

developed the conservatory would house a breeding facility, display animals in their natural habitat, have parking, picnic areas and concessions.

NHDOT Commissioner Charles P. O'Leary, Jr. responded to the Curious Creatures request and asked them to contact NHDOT again in the July / August, 1994 timeframe because plans for the wetlands mitigation and long range usage had not yet been developed.

There is no indication that this group ever followed up on this letter and, while still in existence today, they offer educational programming at schools, libraries and other events, but do not run an animal conservatory.

Provencher Disputes Property Value

Provencher, dissatisfied with the state's purchase price for his property, continued to dispute the price paid at the eminent domain taking. While the state began plans to incorporate the use of this property into the circumferential project, Provencher took steps to prove his position and contested other actions such as the decision about whether the whole property should be declared an historic district.

Like the state, he decided to get two appraisals of the property, but unlike the state, he chose to use appraisal companies located in the southern tier of New Hampshire.

John M. Crafts, Bedford, New Hampshire valued the property, at the time of the eminent domain taking, at $4,950,000, which was significantly higher than what the state paid. Crafts used four comparison sales that ranged from $27,000 to $45,000 per acre. According to his completed appraisal, he felt that the property fell into this price range because Hudson zoning would allow commercial, industrial or residential usage of the property. One of his estimates was $30,000 per acre or $4,975,000. But he didn't stop there. Next he compared against industrial and commercial sales. His final estimate for the property was $4,950,000.

Provencher also contacted a Nashua firm to do his second appraisal and Robert G. Bramley answered his call. Bramley, using the same methodology as Crafts, felt the property was worth even more. According to this appraisal there were both commercial and residential usage possibilities on the property. The commercial acreage was appraised at $135,000 per acre and the residential acreage was appraised at $33,800 per acre. Both prices were given for the time of the eminent domain taking. With Bramley's appraisal, the total appraised price reached $5,600,000.

New Hampshire law defines the steps to be taken when a property appraisal is disputed and Provencher began that process.

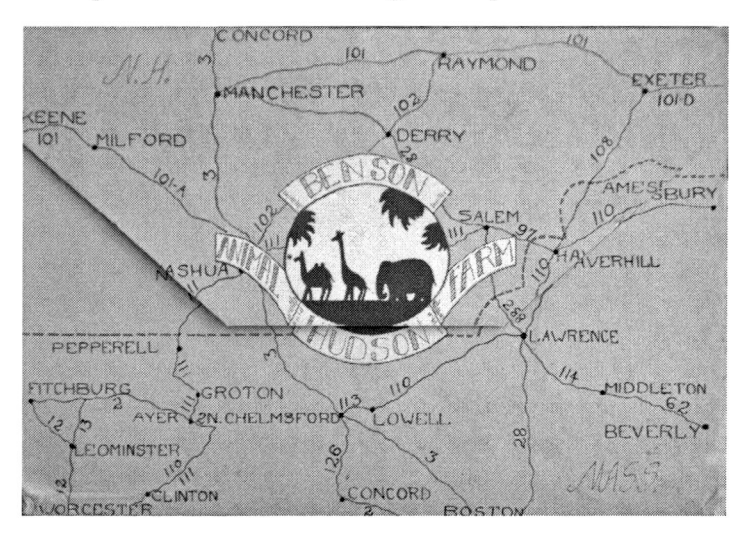

The first step was to request a hearing by the New Hampshire Board of Tax and Land appeals. NHDOT Administrator Murray wrote a letter to J. Cameron Stuart Loan Liquidation Specialist, US Small Bus. Administration stating a hearing on the "appeal of damages by Mr. Provencher in connection with state's eminent domain taking of his land in Hudson. The hearing is set to be July 14 in Hills County Courthouse."

During that hearing both Provencher and the state presented their testimony supporting their positions. After the board heard the testimony, it deliberated. When the results were released, damages had been awarded to Provencher in the amount of $3,700,000. That was still far below the appraisals that Provencher had obtained so he took the next step and filed an appeal. The case would next be heard in the New Hampshire Superior Court.

Eminent Domain Taking Completed
The state filed a Notice of Condemnation with the Hillsborough County Registrar of Deeds on January 24, 1994. This document said, it was for "taking fee simple title to certain property in town of Hudson owned by Arthur Provencher subject to mortgages and liens held by US

Small Business Administration and other lien holders." It was for the entire 165.8 acres previously owned by Provencher. The taking was complete, but the price was still disputed.

Later in 1994, the appeal was heard by a jury. During the trial, all four appraisers testified. Provencher pursued his belief that the price was too low.

The jury heard that 22.5 acres in Amherst, New Hampshire sold to Wal-Mart for $129,378 per acre for a total price of $2,911,000, which was more than the state had paid for the entire Benson property. Wal-Mart also bought a 17.6 acre property in Concord. This smaller property sold for $191,648 per acre for a total of $3,373,000. During the trial questions were asked about why a Concord appraiser for the state made such a low estimate given the two Wal-Mart purchases.

After two days of jury deliberations, the jury released its findings. They found that the 30 acre commercial property along Route 111 was worth $110,000 per acre. The remaining 135.8 acres were deemed to be worth $6,500 per acre. This brought the purchase price to $4,182,700. The jury also awarded that interest in the amount of $692,204.46 be paid and said Provencher's costs in the amount of $11,398 be paid by the state. This total award of $4,886,302.46 minus the original and already paid price of $1,075,000 meant that Provencher received another $3,811,302.46 for his property.

On August 10, 1994, the Department of Justice wrote to NHDOT Commissioner O'Leary, "The Eminent Domain Case was heard and decided by a jury in Superior Court of the Southern District of Hillsborough County." Written confirmation of the jury award in the amount of $4,189,700 for the eminent domain taking was provided and O'Leary was told, "The landowners and their appraisers valued the property at between $5 million and $7 million. The jury verdict is a final and binding obligation on the state, which must be paid."

State Owned Years

Between 1994 and 1997 the state continued to work on projects, including the circumferential highway project. Benson's fell from the public eye. The fence still circled the property, but vandals cut through the fence and visited the property. Buildings were spray painted. The harsh New England weather continued to batter the property and slowly erode the buildings. The state made no attempt to maintain the buildings or the property. Invasive vines began to cover the once-cleared areas and fast growing shrubs and trees formed dense foliage on the property.

The state was fully committed at this point to a partial build of the circumferential highway and permitting, which began in 1993, continued. Even a partial build would alleviate severe traffic problems in Nashua and Hudson and both communities continued to support this project even while residents made jokes about not living to see the project completed. In 1999, nearly 50 years after it was first conceived, the state put the partial build of the circumferential highway into the state's Ten Year Highway Plan.

Establishment of Benson's Historic District
NHDOT had consultants evaluate the Benson property after the eminent domain taking was complete. While the asbestos finding was unpleasant, there were some pleasant aspects. One of those was the recognition of the historic value of the property.

In November 1992, Lynne Emerson Monroe of the Preservation Company, Kensington, NH completed an extensive historic structures survey for New Hampshire Division of Historic Resources [NHDHR]. The findings confirmed that 25 structures on the property were eligible under three of the four National Register of Historic Places criteria to be deemed an historic district. On March 23, 1993 in response to a "Determination of Eligibility for Benson's requested by Arthur Provencher, NHDOT determined that only the area used by Benson would be designated an historic area. This included the area with the buildings and paved walkways and cleared the way for the state to use up to 44 acres for wetlands mitigation for the circumferential highway project.

The merry-go-round at Benson's Wild Animal Farm.

 Finally on May 19, 1994, an official Memorandum of Agreement between NHDOT and the Corps of Army Engineers, a federal agency responsible for a variety of services including adjudicating disputes over historic structures and districts. This agreement outlined the 27 acre Benson Wild Animal Farm Historic District and confirmed that this portion of the property was not to be included in the wetlands mitigation plan.
 This 27 acre parcel sat untouched for years as NHDOT worked on their project. Although the buildings and area had been declared historic, no attempt was made to preserve the area or the structures.

Can we have the train depot?

In 1995 David Alukonis, President Hudson Historical Society, approached Hudson Selectmen and asked if the historical society would ask the state for the old train depot currently sitting on the Benson property. This was the original train depot built for Hudson. It had been moved to Benson's when Hudson no longer needed a train station. The historical society proposed turning it into a museum used to display pieces of Hudson's history. Selectmen readily agreed and offered to help. Alukonis wrote to the NHDOT Commissioner requesting the train depot be transferred to Hudson.

Alukonis said that he never received a reply to this request, but thought the request would be considered when the state was ready to file its plans. Instead everyone was surprised to hear three years later that the state planned to demolish the buildings in the designated historic district.

Vintage Postcard

Prior to a September, 1997 Clean Up Conference for Benson's property, another review was made of the Benson site. At this time NHDHR completed the review and found the designated historic district to be no longer eligible as a district for the National Register due to the loss of integrity through physical decay, vandalism and evidence of post-1947 alterations to the structures. Removal of 16 structures and several animal pens was approved by NHDHR and completed by NHDOT.

The Clean Up conference's purpose was to identify what needed to be done to eliminate hazards, provide security, provide better property management and clean up the debris that had accumulated. Perhaps this led to Nancy Mayville's January, 1998 demolition memo, which proposed to remove the remaining structures.

Demolition Proposed on the property

By January 31, 1998 Nancy Mayville, NHDOT, hand wrote a memo to Lennart at Design Contracts about needed demolition on the Benson property, citing risk and safety concerns. At that time replacement of these seven buildings was estimated to be a total of $360,000 and the contracted needed to produce a risk insurance policy in order to proceed with the

Old ticket booth suffered decay over the years and will be restored as part of Eagle Scout project as Hudson works to open the park to the public.

demo. At the time, the state was looking at the Hazelton Barn on Bush Hill with a replacement value of $90,000, the big main barn also with a replacement value of $90,000, the log cabin with a replacement value of $50,000, the A-Frame food building with a replacement value of $25,000, the gorilla building with a replacement value of $35,000 and the Old Woman's Shoe with a replacement value of $20,000.

On May 5, 1998 a letter was sent to Alukonis indicating that the depot was scheduled for demolition because it had been vandalized and was not secure. This letter acknowledged that in 1995 the Hudson Historical Society had requested the depot be given to them and indicated that if this was still so, the depot needed to be moved before demolition began.

In response, on May 27, 1998 Board of Selectmen Chairman Lorraine Madison followed up on this request and wrote a letter to Nancy Mayville requesting that the depot be given to the historical society and moved. Alukonis said selectmen and historical society were in agreement that the depot should remain in the center of town and were hoping to have it moved to a central location.

No response was received until July 17, 1998 when Hudson Town Administrator Paul Sharon received a letter indicating that the buildings in the Benson Historic District were going to be demolished.

But, the buildings were not demolished. Alukonis says he was never told why nor did he or town officials receive any other communication about moving the depot so it stayed on the Benson property where it still sits in 2010 as this book is being written.

New Amusement Park

In 1997 CMAB Associates, who were associated with Canobie Lake Park, made a proposal to turn much of the Benson property into an amusement park. The law firm of Stebbins, Lazos and Van Der Beken represented CMAB Associates in this effort.

At the time NHDOT wanted to make road improvements at a busy intersection in Salem, NH, which required acquisition of property owned by CMAB Associates, who proposed to swap the Salem land valued at $475,000 for a parcel on the Benson property. Letters from Stebbins, Lazos and Van Der Beken written in May and June of 1992 to Nancy Mayville indicated how the land swap would work and who would be benefited, but as before, final plans had not been developed and the state was reluctant to take any action until those plans were finalized and approved. The intersection was ultimately developed without a land swap.

Barn Burns

A fire burned the remnants of John Benson's homestead and his barn, located on Kimball Hill Road, to the ground on November 24, 1998. The four level barn, built when Benson began sheltering animals on the property, long before Benson's Strangest Farm on Earth opened, had been used to house a restaurant and offices while Benson's was in operation.

David Alukonis recalled that the barn was the oldest of the surviving Benson's buildings. The homestead had been deemed to have no historical value and had been torn down earlier in the year leaving the barn standing on the property.

The suspicious blaze started about 3:45 in the morning. Hudson, Litchfield, Pelham, Windham, Nashua, and Londonderry fire departments responded to the fire. By the time firefighters arrived, it was fully engulfed in flames.

Selectman and volunteer firefighter, Shawn Jasper, saw the blaze while on his way to the fire station. He saw a glow in the sky from Robinson Pond, but by the time he got there, all that was left of the historic barn was timbers and a few flames. He characterized the site as both sort of pretty, but also very sad.

Within two days officials were asking for help in finding out who torched the old barn, which the state had started restoring. At the time of the fire, the barn was part of a controversy involving a development that used Bush Hill Road as its primary access. Thurston's Landing housing development would produce enough traffic that Bush Hill Road had been deemed unsafe unless improvements were made. The developer, the town and NHDOT had been looking at several plans, which required at least 8,000 square feet of one resident's property. However, if the historic barn did not exist, other alternatives for road expansion became viable.

It seemed entirely too convenient that the burn burned to the ground.

The Future

By the end of 1998 Hudson no one was expecting the circumferential highway construction to start and residents were waiting for the state to make that announcement. Residents found ways to deal with the traffic without a by-pass and the future looked bleak for the old Benson property.

Chapter 9

Benson's Future Improves

Long after NHDOT had given up any hope of building any part of this project, the project lingered on the state's Ten Year Highway Plan and its presence there seemed to mock Hudson's efforts to acquire Benson's. After fifty years, the end of the circumferential highway project came not with a bang, but as an almost unnoticed death. Finally control of the Benson property was given to Hudson.

Town Work At Benson's
In 2001 Hudson assumed control of the property and thought the purchase would be finalized soon, selectmen formed a Benson's Committee and began making plans for opening the park as a passive recreation park. No one knew years would pass before the property would change hands.

At the time Selectman Ann Seabury cynically said the committee was formed so that residents would think something was being done.

Selectman Shawn Jasper countered that the committee would work on how the passive park should look when it was finally open.

And work they did. Laurie Jasper, committee secretary, prepared a number of documents. She wrote, "The Committee worked with representatives from NHDOT, Nashua Regional Planning Commission, The Town and the firm of Vanasse, Hangen, Brustlin, Inc (VHB) and developed the Benson's Property Master Plan, which was presented to the Hudson Board of Selectmen. The Benson's Property Master Plan was accepted by a unanimous vote of the Selectmen on that same date and sent to the Planning Board for consideration as an amendment to the Town of Hudson 1996 Master Plan."

In December, 2001 members of the Benson's Committee, wanting to halt the deterioration of the depot and preserve other historic buildings on the land, met with selectmen. Committee member Curt Laffin said that the buildings had been severely damaged and noted that the committee wanted to preserve six structures: a former office building, the Haselton Barn, built in the 18th century, the railroad station, a gorilla cage, the elephant barn and the Old Woman in the Shoe. "Everything was pretty badly vandalized," Laffin announced.

Souvenir Plate

Hudson police bought an all-terrain vehicle to help patrol the land, but Laffin asked for more assistance. Road agent Kevin Burns prepared some of the buildings for winter by boarding them up and taking other precautionary measures and was going to evaluate what other measures should be taken. Historic studies were completed and bickering over how the property had to be maintained began and continued right up to the time that the deed was transferred.

Agreement to Sell

Carol Murray, who worked on this project since the eminent domain taking, received a memo from CORD [Council of Resource Development] on July 25, 2002 that agreed to sell the property to Hudson for $188,000. While the people in Hudson were ecstatic, the state must have had mixed feelings. Things looked promising for Hudson, but the state was facing a loss of millions of dollars since they had lost their court case with Provencher after the eminent domain lawsuit was settled in court.

Asbestos Lawsuit

In December, 2002 news broke that NHDOT had sued George R. Cairns and Sons, who had been hired to work on the wetlands mitigation being done on the Benson's property. The state alleged the company had either brought asbestos contaminated soil to the property from an offsite location or failed to inspect the existing soil before beginning work.

Cairns and Sons fired back, denying any wrong-doing and claiming the asbestos had been there and the state, responsible for removing it, failed to remove the contamination.

NHDOT wanted the contractor to remediate approximately four acres on the property and to reconstruct the wetlands. "As a result of the defendant's negligence, approximately four acres of the Benson's site ... are contaminated with asbestos, which now must be removed, disposed and reconstructed," said the suit paperwork.

Murray announced that she did not want to transfer ownership of the property to Hudson until the suit was settled.

Cairns and Son claimed they had always worked under the watchful eye of state workers, did not have the skills or resources to remove asbestos and did not believe they caused the problem. It was obvious this would drag through court and Hudson would wait until the suit was settled out of court a number of years later.

Park Stabilization

In 2003, selectmen awarded three contracts for work to weatherize and stabilize several buildings at the former amusement park using money approved by voters. With these awards some preservation of the existing buildings began.

The contracts included $27,900 for Preservation Timber Framing Inc. to stabilize the barn, including sealing all the entrances, such as windows and doors and removing some debris inside the barn.

Contracts for roofing repairs and work on a kitchen and train depot and for other work on those areas were also awarded. At the time Town Administrator Steve Malizia said there was some asbestos abatement work also needed and noted some ceiling tiles would be removed.

Old ticket booth shows decay after years of neglect under state ownership. However, soon a Boy Scout Eagle project will begin to refurbish the booth.

The total cost of the three contracts was $53,700. Fortunately Hudson voters had established a fund for Benson's during a town election. The money needed for the work came from this fun. Voters had approved a total $253,000 for the preservation and development of Benson's property.

Bones Found During Preservation
Dunne's Demolition and Asbestos Removal was the vendor chosen to work on the kitchen and gift shop. This would include asbestos removal in this structure as well as to restoration of a roof of another nearby building.

On December 26, 2003 demolition workers got a shock when a skull rolled out of a wall in one of the property's old buildings. Juan Felix, a supervisor for the company, said he and another worker were attempting to pull out some ductwork from a wall when several bones fell out of a cylinder leading to an exhaust fan. The men were working on the gift shop and the attached kitchen that at one time led to the "Bavarian Beer Garden" at the former amusement park.

Felix called owner Tim Dunne and told him they had found a small body, perhaps a baby. Dunne told his men to stop work, not touch anything and said he would call the police, who responded in record time arriving at 12:55 p.m.

Police Sergeant Bob Tousignant led the team that photographed and carefully removed the remains, which were sent to the state lab. After analysis, the bones were determined to be animal – probably belonging to a monkey.

Esther McGraw, Benson's Committee, later said monkeys were on the park, but the pens had not been near this building.

Felix said that he was used to finding things, but it was the first time that he'd ever found bones during a demolition.

Purchase Price to Go Up?

Years passed and Hudson still didn't own the park. During their televised meetings selectmen discussed the generalities of the lagging Benson purchase, but declined to give specifics because they were in "negotiations."

In 2007 selectmen warned they would back out of the Benson's land deal if the state insisted the town meet federal historical building standards in the renovation and maintenance of two buildings on the site and further said they wouldn't take ownership of an aging barn if the state insisted on subjecting the building to federal historical preservation guidelines as part of the town's deal to purchase the sprawling property.

At the heart of the last dispute was a state requirement that the buildings in the area formerly designated as a historic site be preserved historically. Hudson pointed out that the state allowed the buildings to deteriorate so much under their care that the "historic site" was no longer eligible for the National Register and that such maintenance would cost millions of dollars – dollars the town didn't have nor planned to raise.

Town Counsel Jay Hodes sent a letter to the Division of Historical Resources asking that they reconsider requiring the town to follow costly federal guidelines for renovating the nearly 200-year-old Haselton Barn.

Nearly a year later in April 2008 the state announced it planned to re-appraise the Benson property and set a fair market value for purchase. Hudson residents thought a purchase and sales agreed with a set price had already been signed. There was community outrage.

Was this another negotiating ploy or had the state merely been trying to out-wait Hudson? It was clear to all that the agreed upon purchase price was well below market value and millions of dollars less than the state's purchase price for the property. Was this the reason that the sale hadn't been completed?

Some felt the state had been holding up the final sale. First a lawsuit against a vendor, then requirements for historical preservation of decayed buildings and now a re-appraisal of the land that all acknowledged was worth more than the agreed upon sale price.

Selectman Shawn Jasper called the action highly unethical.

That April, Jeff Brillhart, NHDOT Assistant Commissioner, denied that the state was considering selling the land to a developer, but said the new appraisal would likely mean a higher sales price for the town.

Brillhart said the site would be assessed without the wetland restrictions that reduced its value when the state bought as part of the planned circumferential highway. At this time the town assessor's office valued the property at $3.6 million.

By July, 2008 the remaining obstacle to finalizing the purchase, seemed to be the 18th century Haselton Barn, which was originally part of the Haselton Farm. It was agreed many barns built in the 18th century had deteriorated before collapsing, and that it was unusual that this barn was still standing. Selectmen didn't believe they should be charged with historical preservation on a building that had not been maintained.

"It's not that we're not willing to preserve the buildings, we just want to make sure it's done at a reasonable price," Jasper said.

By July, 2008 selectmen tried a new tactic by agreeing to, but not signing a deed that outlined the terms of the purchase of the property from NHDOT. Town attorney, Jay Hodes, forwarded the deed to DOT officials. The back and forth continued.

Finally Selectman Roger Coutu picked up the phone, called NHDOT and asked when the deed would be signed.

Amazingly in January, 2009, Hudson finally owned the Benson property. Selectmen and too many volunteers to count began and continue to work on this property. As the book goes to press, the grand opening, planned for Memorial Day weekend, 2010, for Benson Park draws closer.

Plans for a new Park

The Selectman appointed Benson Committee swung into action. Buildings began to be refurbished; brush cleaned and debris discarded. Volunteers came out to help and monthly work sessions were established.

Community groups have offered to work on the park, which will be opened May 29, 2010. The Hudson Community Club and its sister club, the Juniors, got approval for a butterfly garden and have been removing trees and other debris from their plot.

Benson wagon part of Benson memorabilia exhibit held shortly after town acquired the property.

A dog park is being discussed. Another group wants to build football fields. Trails are being opened and Boy Scouts are developing Eagle projects that will help the park.

The park has been officially named Benson Park and will offer picnicking and other passive recreational opportunities.

Once again people asking directions will hear, "Do you know where Benson's is?"

Bibliography

A Butterfly Garden at Benson Park by Lynne Ober, ANG, 2010.
A Visit to Benson Wild Animal Farm by Eddie Jackson, SPEC, Vol 1, No. 3 1940, pg 4
A Lot More to Buy the Farm? The Nashua Telegraph April 30, 2008
Al Jones
Amy Laffin
Benson Animal Farm, by Anne Lundregan, The Nashua Telegraph, October 26, 2001
Benson's Historic Structures Report, Town of Hudson, January 31, 2003
Benson's land sale still not complete, but talks ongoing, by Joseph Cote, The Nashua Telegraph, September 2, 2008
Benson's Project Garners Award, Neighbor's section, The Nashua Telegraph, July, 26, 2004
Bob Lovejoy
Bret Bronson
Carnegie Hero Fund Commission medal www.carnegiehero.com.
Colossus - A Swing for the White House, by Cynthia Jones, Nashua Telegraph
Couple loses latest round in fight to run exotic zoo, staff and wire, The Nashua Telegraph, December 11, 1998
Curt Laffin
David Alukonis
Death Takes John T. Benson, Wild Animal Authority, September 20, 1943, Nashua Telegraph
Esther McGraw
http://bucklesw.blogspot.com
http://bucklesw.blogspot.com/2007/11/roland-tiebor.html
Hudson Historical Society documents and photos
Hudson Historically Speaking by Diane Chubb and Lynne Ober, History Press, 2009
Hudson Moves Closer to Bensons Acquisition by Gina M. Votour, Area News Group
John Ferbert
John Simo

Laurie Jasper document for the town of Hudson. Found at http://www.ci.hudson.nh.us/boards/documents/bensons-LJasper.pdf
Lucille Boucher
Nashua Telegraph (May 25, 1974) Dean Shalhoup "Benson's Features Gorilla, Varied Acts, Attractions"
New Hampshire Department of Transportation: 1992-2002 Architectural Study of Benson's Animal Farm
NH Department of Transportation Files on Benson's Wild Animal Park
Rare Sights at Benson's Animal Farm, June 4, 1927 Nashua Telegraph
Remembering Benson's Wild Animal Farm, by Bob Goldsack, 1998
Ruth Parker
Sue Hoadley
Sue Mizek
The Lowell Sun "To Decide Norumbega Park Fate" April 10, 1961
Wild times in old Hudson Center, The Nashua Telegraph, by Dean Shalhoup, September 3, 1995
William Gardner, New Hampshire Secretary of State
Winter Stabilization, by Anne Lundregan, The Nashua Telegraph, December 2, 2003
Woburn: A Past Observed, John McElhiney

About the Author

Lynne Ober is currently serving a third term as New Hampshire State Representative and also teaches in the Computer Information Science program at the University of New Hampshire. Combining her love of photography and writing, she is an active freelance writer and photographer. Lynne and her husband, Russ, have lived in Europe and Asia. She is a longtime member of the Hudson Historical Society and served on its board of directors. She also served six years on Hudson's School Board and was the Hudson School Board representative to the Budget Committee for six years. She is a member of the Friends of the Library and the VFW Auxiliary. In addition, she volunteers for a variety of town activities, including volunteering with the committee trying to open the former Benson's Wild Animal Farm as a park and Hudson Old Home Days Celebration. She recently became a member of the board of directors of the Friends of Benson, a non-profit corporation formed to raise funds for the park restoration. An avid gardener, she established gardens at Kimball Webster School, which houses the Hudson School District superintendent and is currently working to establish a butterfly garden at Benson Park.